A COUNTRY TREASURY

A COUNTRY

TREASURY

Edited by Allen D. Bragdon

Foreword by Dr. Robert Bishop, Director,
Museum of American Folk Art

Acknowledgments

This work was inspired by many generations of folk artists and craftspeople. It was conceived and produced by Allen D. Bragdon Publishers, Inc. The following people contributed their skills, ideas, and objects from their collections:

Editors and Writers: Barbara Benton, Janet Clark, Ann Maxwell, Bernd Metz, Don Nelson (senior writer), Paula Reedy, Hannah Selby, Cecelia K. Toth, M.C. Waldrep

Project Craftspeople: Ed and Stevie Baldwin, Yvonne Bell, Christine Brandl, Andrew Clements, Joan Endres, Marsha Evans Moore, Meg Shinnal and Kathy Bryant of Ginnie Thompson Originals, Valentina Snell, Dorothy Sparling, Carla van Arnam

Photographers: Douglas Foulke, Charles Gold, Robert Goldwitz, Marion Ham, Richard Jeffrey, Myron Miller, Neil Portnoy

Graphics: Ed Lipinsky (full-color illustrations), John Miller (design), Stephanie Schaffer (art direction), Bernie Springsteel (layout), Carol Winter (two-color illustrations)

Recipes: Joanna Bragdon, Martha Custis, Tammy Nathan, and Alice Reid. Contributors to *The Artist in the Kitchen*, published by the Saint Louis Art Museum: Mrs. Frank J. Bush, Jr., Mrs. Jean-Jacques Carnal, Olita Lloyd Davis, Mrs. Mary Eigel, Mrs. Jack Randall, Mrs. Harry O. Schloss, Mrs. Joan A. Wattenberg, Charles Whitten

Food and Styling: Sherry McGlodrick of Karo corn syrup (gingerbread, carolers centerpieces); Desserts by Michelle and Daughter, New York (all other desserts); Yvonne McHarg (styling, antiques)

Owners of Objects Photographed: Edward Abrams, American Antiques & Accents, Langhorne, PA; Joanna Bragdon, Cape Cod, MA; Robert Brandegee, Pittsburgh, PA; Concord Fabrics, Concord, NY; Thomas and Pamela Cushman, Yarmouth, ME; Phyllis Haders, NY; Hammer & Hammer, American Folk Art, Chicago, IL; Roberta and Rebecca Jorgensen, R. Jorgensen Antiques, Wells, ME; Bettie Mintz, All of Us Americans Folk Art, Bethesda, MD; Mt. Vernon Ladies Assoc., Mt. Vernon, VI; New York State Historical Assoc., Cooperstown; Price Glover, Inc., NY; Virginia Ramsey-Pope, Dorset, VT; Sheila and Edwin Rideout, Sheila Rideout Antiques, Woodbury, CT; Rita Rodwell, Pawley's Island, NC; St. Regis Paper Co., NY; Steve's Antiques, NY; Meryl Weiss, American Classics, NY; Mr. and Mrs. Nate Wallace, Willowdale Antiques, Kennett Square, PA

Martha Washington's Great Cake Recipe on page 147 ©American Heritage Publishing Co. Inc., reprinted by permission from American Heritage Cookbook and Illustrated History of American Eating.

A Brownstone Library Book

Edited, Designed and Produced by
Allen D. Bragdon Publishers, Inc.
252 Great Western Road
South Yarmouth, MA 02664

Originally published by Allen D. Bragdon Publishers, Inc. under the title
A Country Christmas Treasury

This edition published in 1995 by
SMITHMARK Publishers, Inc.,
16 East 32nd Street
New York, NY 10016

SMITHMARK books are available for bulk purchase for sales promotion and premium use. For details write or call the manager of special sales, SMITHMARK Publishers, Inc., 16 East 32nd Street, New York, NY 10016 (212) 532-6600.

Library of Congress Cataloging in Publication Data
Main entry under title:
A Country Treasury
   1. Christmas decorations. 2. Christmas cookery.
3. Christmas. I. Bragdon, Allen D.
TT900. C4C68 1983 745.594'1 83-11776

ISBN 0-8317-1434-4

Printed in Korea
10 9 8 7 6 5 4 3 2 1

Contents

Foreword

Crafting things by hand has never frightened Americans. The earliest settlers came to a strange coastal frontier, then pressed westward using what was available, making do with what they could get, or doing without. Those people brought skills and designs from their own countries that established and have continuously nourished a new folk culture. In the 200 years since its beginnings this huge land has attracted people who were willing to go it alone to make their way. Artisans who were willing to work—to put the time into something they cared about doing well—have enriched their adopted folk heritage as they have made their way from immigrants to property owners. Much of American folk art reflects these national qualities of resourcefulness, invention, and individuality.

Those are still our strengths. We live more urban lives now, though, with packaged entertainments available to fill our leisure. Although we are tempted to buy the newest thing and get another when it breaks, the long evenings are still there, as they were when the daylight to work by was gone or the store closed for the night. In these pieces of private time many people still, after the chores or Sunday dinner, pick up the basket of fabric scraps to cut and stitch a little more on a sewing project; or they disappear into the shop to work a piece of stock that fits into a design idea they are gradually shaping. Like the best of our antique folk art, each object is being made with patience and exacting care—ripped out and started over if it's not just right. More than likely those projects are for another's comfort or delight: a toy, for example, that the child is likely to remember all his life but equally likely to forget where it came from. Again, like good folk art, because they were designed with thought and made with care, these objects will last long enough to pass down and become antiques.

Folk art tends to appeal to all kinds of people with different varieties of experiences and education. Perhaps one reason for this fact is that folk designs have been good enough to last, to be repeated, to be borrowed and adapted by others in a personal way. They may be whimsical, spare, intricately patterned, utilitarian, fresh, or weathered—but something about them is appealing. Perhaps their appeal is simply that they are *not* new, that they have survived to give us a glimpse of the lives of those who came before us. Sometimes when we hold a fine piece of antique folk art in our hands we can't help but wonder what was in the mind of its maker when he or she first thought it through and began to work on it.

The designs for the decorations, gifts, and toys to be made from the instructions in this book were copied or adapted from old works of American folk art. Recreating the old pieces uses many of the same techniques—rug braiding, quilting, carpentry, embroidery—as the original artist-craftsperson used; but, fortunately, these adaptations do not always require the same degree of skilled experience. They couldn't. Most of the objects of original folk art pictured in this book are the works of masters who either made them for a living or spent months making them out of necessity. Not everybody today, or yesterday for that matter, has the experience or the time to make objects as demanding as most of those original designs. But many of the contemporary projects for which instructions are given here have been adapted from the original materials or size, so they can more easily be made without special skills. These designs are both traditional and practical. They may be copied exactly or adapted by the imagination of the maker, but if the materials are skillfully wrought these works will last and may be valued by those who come after us as we now cherish folk objects and traditions from the past.

Dr. Robert Bishop, Director
American Museum of Folk Art

TRIMMINGS

When the first snow falls and the Christmas season begins, the home becomes the center of family life more than at any other time of year. Friends and family—aunts and uncles you see only once a year, neighbors you greet every day, brothers and sisters you've spent other Christmases with when you were growing up—gather to share in the festivities. The joyful warmth and spirit of your home help create a holiday atmosphere to be remembered and recreated year after year with old family and traditions and fresh surprises.

The home trimmings included in this section celebrate nature and the spirit of Christmas in the simple and bountiful atmosphere of rural life. The materials come mostly from nature, the designs from our country folk heritage, and the making of them becomes a happy blend of giving and receiving.

Everyone can participate in creating these projects. Children can go out before the first snowfall to collect pinecones and evergreen boughs for wreaths, and centerpieces. Someone might stitch up some calico ornaments one long autumn evening or bake a gingerbread centerpiece. Just before the holidays it will be time to string popcorn and cranberries and together make the decorations that make a holiday memorable.

Christmas tree ornaments have a way of collecting associations with the person who brought them into the collection or the year they were added. Many among these largely Victorian examples have been handed down for more than three generations.

Chapter 1: Decorations

Peppermint Wreath

This is a fun holiday decoration to brighten up your home with, and it's fairly simple to construct. The only hard part is avoiding the temptation to eat the basic material needed to make the wreath!

Materials and tools

80–100 red-and-white-striped mint candies.
3½′ of 2″–2½″-wide red velveteen or satin ribbon.
Several yds. of white string.
Red electrical tape.
2′ of silver ribbon or string.
6″-piece of thin wire.
1 wire coat hanger.
Wire cutters.
A pair of children's scissors.

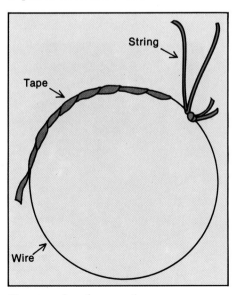

Constructing the wreath

1. Remove the hook from the coat hanger. Form hanger into a circle six in. in diameter. Bind the ends together, cutting off any excess wire. Wrap the entire hanger in the red tape.

2. Tie two pieces of string together to any point in the hanger, as shown.
3. Near the knot, form a loop from one of the pieces of string; slip in one end of a candy wrapper and tighten the knot.
4. Wrap the second piece of string around the other side of the candy wrapper, and partially around the wire as well, holding it tight.

5. Continuing in the direction of the second piece of string, alternately repeat Steps 3 and 4 until all but two in. of the wire ring is covered with the candies. Crowd the candies as close together as possible.
6. Knot the string.

Making the bow

1. Cut a 3¼-in. piece of red ribbon.

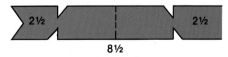

2. Place the ribbon face down and fold it from left to right, stopping at the dotted line (marked "8½" in the figure).
3. Keep folding the ribbon from left to right, gathering it at the indentations indicated to form a bow with four loops and two tails.
4. Fasten the center of the bow with thin wire, leaving the wire's ends loose at the back of the bow.

5. Cut a strip of ribbon, 3 in. by ¾ in., and fold in half lengthwise. Attach it around the center of the bow to conceal the wire. Fasten the ribbon in the rear with the same wire, leaving the wire ends loose.
6. Attach the bow to the 2-in. area on the wreath that is uncovered; the silver loop should hang behind, in the center of the bow. Cut off or fasten the loose ends of the wire.

Attaching the ribbon

1. Cut the silver ribbon into two 1-ft. pieces, forming each into a circle; knot.
2. Wind one piece of ribbon around the scissors' handle; form a loop and slip the other end of the circle through it, pulling tight.

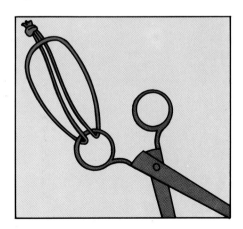

3. In the same manner, loop the scissors to the bottom of the wreath, opposite the bow, so that they dangle downward.
4. Attach the second silver ring to the top of the wreath, in the center of the two-in. gap. Use this loop to suspend the wreath.

Evergreen roping—interspersed with deciduous fronds—and ribbons gives an easier, country feeling to this Colonial hallway than formal Victorian roping would. Note the sleigh bells on the newel post and the old hooked rug.

A few generations ago, every boy longed to find a little red wagon under his Christmas tree, and it remained his treasured possession long after he stopped playing in it.

A traditional evergreen wreath, highlighted with bright bows, brings holiday colors and the refreshing aroma of pine into the home at Christmas.

 # Evergreen Wreath

Fill your home with the fragrance of Christmas as you deck the halls, mantel, staircase, and front door with evergreen.

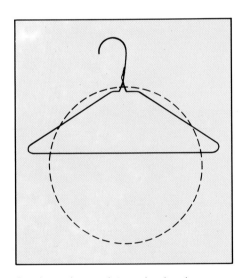

Bend coat hanger into a circular shape.

Wire the sprigs onto the hanger, near the top.

Roping illustrated without needles, for clarity.

Materials and tools

Wire coat hanger (for wreath).
Large quantity of evergreen sprigs (24 of 6″ x 12″ lengths for wreath).
Several spools of florist wire.
Pine cones or crab apples (for wreath).
2 yds. of wide red ribbon (for wreath).
Wire cutter.
Scissors

Constructing the wreath

1. Bend the coat hanger so that it forms a circle, leaving the hook on.
2. Wire the ends of two or three bunches of sprigs onto the hanger, near the top.
3. Continue wiring the bunches onto the hanger frame, making sure they lie in the same direction.
4. When the wreath is finished, snip off protruding ends of the wire, and even up the wreath's shape by trimming the greens with scissors.
5. For instructions for making the bows, see the wrapping project in this chapter. Make twelve or fifteen small bows and attach them to the wreath with the tail ends of the wire that holds the bow together. You can also attach two or three larger bows instead.

For roping

1. Lay out the sprigs so that they overlap, then wire them together.
2. Continue overlapping until desired length is reached.

Grapevine Wreath and Basket

Decorations made of woven vines can be hung indoors or out and last almost indefinitely. The spring and early fall are the best times to gather wild grapevines to make wreaths and baskets. Dead vines or wintering ones will break when you work with them. If your vines seem too brittle immerse them in hot water or soak them overnight to make them bend without breaking.

A few breaks are unavoid able and add to the rustic appearance.

Materials

12′–30′ of leafless, wild grapevine.

Constructing the wreath

1. Determine the size of your wreath. A 12-ft. vine will make a wreath 16 inches in diameter, two or three inches thick. For a thicker wreath, simply increase the length of your vines.

2. Form the wreath into a circle by putting the end of the vine through the center again and again until the entire length is wound up.

3. An alternate way to form the wreath is to loop the vine again and again *without* intertwining it, then tie the wreath at four or five places with twine. When looping the vine this way, it is helpful to wind it inside a waste basket or barrel, which will hold it coiled in place until ready for tying.

4. The wreath can be decorated with seasonal fruit or vegetables, such as small gourds or squash, crab apples, dried peppers, etc., or with bittersweet.

Constructing the Basket

1. To start a basket, coil a long section of vine in an oval shape, interlacing the offshoots to secure the form. Tie the vines with twine here and there as you work. Continue coiling vines until the desired height is reached; tuck all ends in securely.

2. To make oval handles, weave vines down through the sides.

3. To make the bottom, attach a long vine to the inside outer edge with wire, and coil it toward the center; secure it with wire.

4. You may find it necessary to secure parts of the basket with fine florist's wire before cutting the twine away. If you have soaked the vines, let them dry out before cutting the twine.

5. Spray the basket with clear acrylic.

An alternate method

If the vines are still too inflexible after soaking, try this method: nail long spikes through a scrap of lumber to outline the shape you desire. Coil and interlace vines around the spikes, tying them with twine as necessary.

Distelfink Doves with Heart

Materials

¼ yard off-white wool fabric.
Scrap of blue-and-white plaid fabric
Off-white thread.
Polyfill stuffing.

A grapevine basket makes an appropriate setting for a pair of doves, crafted of homespun in the Pennsylvania Dutch distelfink style.

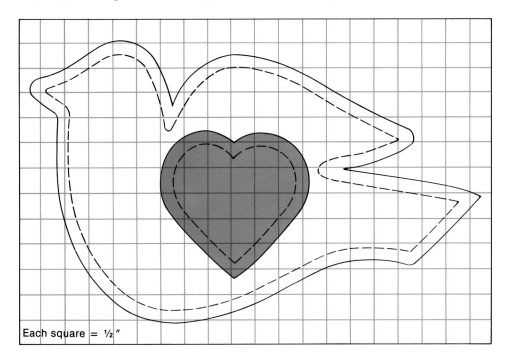

Each square = ½″

Directions

1. Enlarge patterns to full size. From white wool cut 4 doves and one heart. From blue-and-white fabric cut one heart.

2. With right sides in, stitch doves together in pairs, using ¼″ seams and leaving a 2½″ opening at the bottom. With right sides in, stitch hearts together, leaving a small opening near the bottom on one side. Clip and trim seam allowance of all pieces; turn right side out.

3. Stuff doves and heart; slipstitch openings closed.

4. Place doves facing one another with the heart between the beaks. Tack heart to beaks; tack breasts of doves together.

✳ Holly Wreath

"Of all the trees that are in the wood, the holly bears the crown." This project develops a pleasing combination of shapes, colors and contours into the perfect "crown" for door and mantel.

The berries and leaves used are like little pillows. Each shape is stuffed lightly with polyester batting, which gives the wreath its special three dimensional quality.

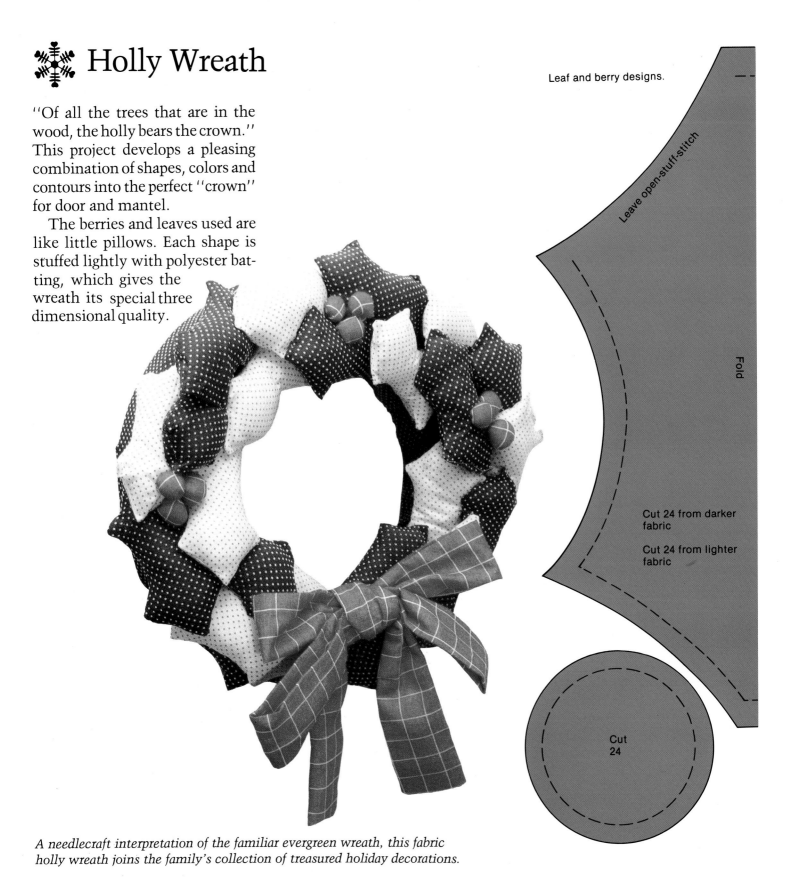

Leaf and berry designs.

Leave open-stuff-stitch

Fold

Cut 24 from darker fabric

Cut 24 from lighter fabric

Cut 24

A needlecraft interpretation of the familiar evergreen wreath, this fabric holly wreath joins the family's collection of treasured holiday decorations.

Materials

½ yd. red print fabric (for bow and berries).
⅔ yd. light fabric (wreath shown has white with green polka dots).
1½ yds. bright fabric (wreath shown has green with white polka dots.)
14″ styrofoam wreath base, or a coat hanger bent into a circle and plumped out with batting or scrap fabric.
½ lb. of polyester quilt batting.
Dressmakers' carbon paper.
Scissors, thread, straight pins.

Preparing the parts

1. Cover the wreath base with the darker fabric. The one shown took a 48 in. by 10 in. piece. Overlap and whipstitch the fabric together on the back side of the wreath.
2. Using the leaf and berry designs, make template-patterns from shirtboard-weight cardboard.
3. Trace and then cut out 24 leaf shapes from the dark fabric and 24 from the light fabric.
4. Make 12 light leaves and 12 dark leaves. Place right sides together and stitch all 24 holly leaves along the dotted lines, leaving the unmarked edge open. Clip the curves, trim the corners and then turn each leaf right side out and press. Stuff lightly with polyester batting and whipstitch the openings closed.

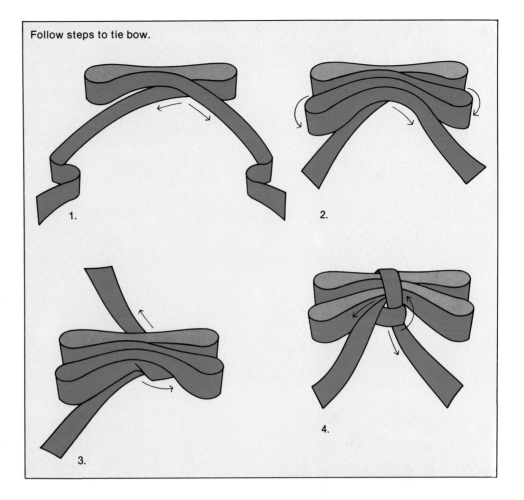

Follow steps to tie bow.

1.

2.

3.

4.

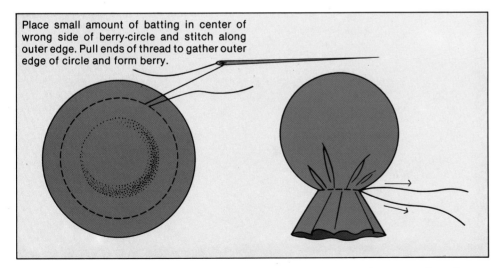

Place small amount of batting in center of wrong side of berry-circle and stitch along outer edge. Pull ends of thread to gather outer edge of circle and form berry.

5. Trace and then cut 12 berry circles out of the red print fabric. Stuff and gather each of the 12 circles along the dotted lines.
6. Piece red print fabric together to make a strip 5½ in. by 38 in. Fold the strip together end-to-end, right side in. Sew along the raw edges, leaving one end open. Turn right side out, press, and whipstitch the end closed. The diagram shows how to tie the bow.

Assembling the wreath

1. Pin 12 leaves, alternating light and dark, along the outer edge of the wreath base. Start at the bottom of the base and make the leaves overlap ends evenly.
2. Pin the remaining 12 leaves along the inner edge of the wreath base. Start at the bottom and make leaves overlap evenly. The outer edges of the inner leaves should also overlap the outer leaves slightly, with light leaves overlapping dark ones and vice versa.
3. When the leaves are all pinned in place correctly, sew them to the fabric covering the wreath base. Each leaf should be tacked to the base fabric in two or three places to hold it in position.
4. Sew the 12 berries together into four bunches of three berries each, and stitch the bunches at even intervals around the wreath.
5. Sew the bow to the bottom of the wreath. Now hang the finished wreath on your front door, pour yourself a glass of eggnog, and wait for the compliments.

Pinecone Creations

These striking pinecone constructions are as typically country as you can get; the raw materials may even be lying in your yard, if you live in pinetree country. All three projects are easy to make, and require no tools. The frames for the wreath and basket are sold at many florists and decorations stores, but you can use "found" objects if you like, such as a discarded round picture frame or small wood or plastic fruit boxes.

A pinecone basket provides the perfect container for holiday decorations, fruits, Christmas gifts, or the family's favorite heirloom toys.

Materials for the Basket

10'' wire basket frame or wire garden basket with feet. (Florists usually stock basket frames in several sizes and shapes.)
Wire coat hanger for handle.
Approximately 4-dozen flat-bottom cones, such as red or pitch (New Jersey) pinecones.
Approximately 100 small cones, such as white spruce, Douglas fir, hemlock, larch, or others.
Electric glue gun, melt glue, or other fast-drying glue.
Clear acrylic spray.

Making the basket

1. To make coat-hanger handle for the basket, cut two lengths for the arch and attach them with pliers. Cut several small pieces and affix them with pliers at intervals to hold the arches apart.

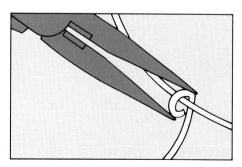

2. Starting at the bottom, insert flat-bottom cones, making sure the basket will stand evenly. Then insert cones on handle and top rim, and fill the area between until the basket form is completely covered.

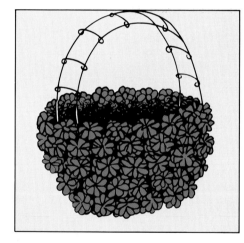

3. Glue small cones to trim the edges of the handle, the rim, and to fill spaces between cones all around the basket.
4. Spray with clear acrylic.

Holiday joy radiates from the face of this little girl who has just arrived at Grandmother's for her first Christmas in the country. Her mother gave her a present before she left home: her dream Christmas dress in red velveteen, trimmed with ribbon, ruffles, and lace. And Grandmother has given her a typical country gift—a pinecone basket, made of cones from the trees that shade the old farmhouse.

Materials for the Door Wreath

16'' tier wire wreath frame.

Approximately 5-dozen white pinecones for background.

Several large Georgia pine or Norway spruce cones for focal points. Cones of different sizes, such as Scotch, ponderosa, pinon, pitch pine, white spruce, Douglas fir, hemlock, etc.

Florist wire.

Electric glue gun or fast-drying glue.

Clear acrylic spray.

Making the wreath

1. Place wire wreath rounded side down.
2. Soak white pinecones in water and place them horizontally inside the wire frame with the tip ends in groups of two or three in opposite directions. Wet pines close but will partially reopen after drying for several days in a warm place, forming a tight, firm base for the wreath.

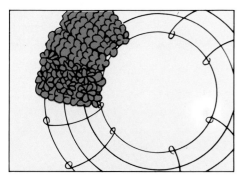

3. When the base is completely dry, wire large cones to the wreath by circling them with wire, pulling the wires to the back, and tying them securely.
4. Fill in areas with assorted cones, using an electric glue gun to secure them. Trim edges with small cones.
5. Spray the wreath with clear acrylic.

Although made of rustic materials, the pinecone door wreath seems to bear a family resemblance to the della Robbia wreaths of the 15th-16th centuries, which also used natural objects, but in a ceramic medium.

The pinecone candle holder is a modern copy of a traditional Christmas decoration brought to this country from Austria many years ago.

Materials for the Candle holder

1 large, squat pinecone, 3'' to 5'' in diameter.

6 or 8 small pinecones or beechnut husks, ½'' in diameter.

8 or 10 short, full-needle sprigs of evergreen.

1 candle.

8'' to 10'' length of florist wire.

White glue.

Penknife.

Silver paint or white flocking (optional).

Making the Candle holder

1. Loop the florist wire twice around the core of the pinecone near the base. Pull the wire out between the cone's layers so that the ends come out of the bottom.

2. Form a nest around the pinecone by tying the ends of the evergreen sprigs to the wire. Snip off excess wire.

3. Cut off the top of the pinecone with the penknife, making a flat area about two inches in diameter. Glue the smaller cones around the edge, to make a circle large enough to hold your candle.

4. The pinecone can be decorated, if you wish, by frosting its edges with silver paint or white flocking.

5. Drip melted wax into the center of the pinecone and mount the candle.

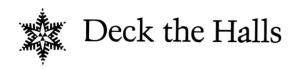

Deck the Halls

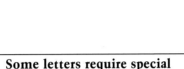

If you're handy with needle and thread and have a few fabric scraps around the house, you can create a holiday wall hanging that distinctively spells out your favorite way of saying Merry Christmas.

Materials

Fabric scraps (reversible if possible).
Fiberfill.
2 small nylon curtain rings.
Sewing machine.
Sewing thread, pins, and scissors.

Designing the hanging

Select a phrase of approximately 20 letters with symbols, such as:
    Deck the Hall—holly leaves.
    O Christmas Tree—tree and presents.
    The First Noel—star and angels.
    'Twas the Night Before Christmas—a mouse and house.
    Joy to the World—star, musical notes.
    Away in a Manger—star and lambs.
    God Bless You, Tiny Tim—presents and tree.

Constructing the letters

1. Draw the letters of each word you've chosen on a piece of paper, making each at least 1½ in. wide. Keep in mind that the size of your letters will determine the overall size of your hanging.
2. Cut each letter out from two layers of fabric.
3. Sew together the edges of each letter-piece, leaving a one- or two-in. opening.
4. Turn each letter right-side-out and stuff with the fiberfill.
5. Finish each letter by whip-stitching the opening.

Some letters require special treatment.

1. The small letter 1 should be sewn around its perimeter *except* at the top, then turned right-side-out and stuffed.
2. For those letters with an inner space (o, a, or e), sew the *outer* perimeter first. Turn right-side-out and whip-stitch the inner perimeter, leaving an inch or two unsewn where it can be stuffed. To finish, whip-stitch the unsewn area.
3. For dotted letters, such as i or j, simply join the dot to the body of the letter.

Constructing the symbols

1. The symbols should correspond in size to the letters. Draw their shapes on paper and cut out.
2. Pin each shape to two pieces of fabric and cut out.
3. With right sides together, sew the edges of each shape, leaving a one- or two-in. opening.
4. Turn shapes right-side-out and stuff to a thickness of ¾-in. Use a whip-stitch to close up each opening.
5. To give the symbols a quilted look, use the sewing machine to stitch details onto each shape.

❄ Gingerbread Farm

Elaborate gingerbread constructions, like the farm on these pages, have been the focal points of Christmas tables, mantel pieces, and under-the-tree decorations for generations. Most of them are a little frustrating for children since, although they're mouth-watering, they're meant only for decoration. This farm solves that problem with a woodshed full of gingerbread logs just for eating.

The traditional gingerbread house, made of tasty cookies and gobs of sweet icing, probably originated with the edible witch's house in "Hansel and Gretel." The patterns and recipes for making this country-farm Christmas centerpiece appear on the following pages; the shapes of the animals are original, not from cookie cutters, so use them as an inspiration to draw your own patterns.

The logs in the woodshed are for big and little fingers to snatch. Make a big batch and freeze some for replacements while your farm is on display during the holiday season.

Cookie Dough (Make recipe three times.)

3½ cups unsifted flour
  1 teaspoon ground cinnamon
  ½ teaspoon ground ginger
  ½ teaspoon ground nutmeg
  ½ teaspoon ground cloves
  ⅛ teaspoon salt
  1 cup corn-oil margarine
  ⅓ cup firmly-packed, light-brown sugar
  ⅔ cup light corn-syrup

1. In a small bowl stir together flour, cinnamon, ginger, nutmeg, cloves, and salt.
2. In a large bowl, using an electric mixer at medium speed, beat margarine to soften. Gradually beat in sugar. Beat in corn-syrup until well-blended. Reduce speed to low; gradually beat in flour mixture until well mixed.
3. Cover; refrigerate several hours.

Decorator Frosting (Make recipe three times, or as needed.)

  1 lb. confectioner's sugar
  3 Egg whites
  ½ teaspoon cream of tartar
    Food colors

1. In a large bowl, with an electric mixer at low speed, beat together confectioner's sugar, egg whites, and cream of tartar until blended.
2. With mixer at high speed, beat 7 to 10 minutes, or until knife drawn through mixture leaves a path.
3. Divide mixture and tint desired colors. Keep covered with damp cloth.
Makes about 2 cups.
NOTE: This frosting will be of a much stiffer consistency when dry than other frosting recipes. This is so it will hold the pieces firmly together.

Preparing the patterns

1. See Skills Pages for instructions on how to enlarge pattern pieces on the opposite page. When you have done this, transfer patterns from tracing paper to lightweight cardboard.
2. Draw the animal figures, farmer, and sleigh to your own fancy on lightweight cardboard. Keep lines (legs, arms, etc.) thick because cookies *do* crumble. Cut out.

Making the pieces

1. Line five 12 × 15½-inch cookie sheets with aluminum foil. Place 2⅓ cups dough on each cookie sheet. (Place damp cloth under cookie sheets or moisten surface under foil to prevent sliding.) Roll out dough to 11 × 15 × ¼-inch rectangle. Cover and refrigerate at least 30 minutes. (If you don't have or can't borrow the 5 sheets needed, roll out the dough on foil and slide foil onto trays or large pieces of cardboard to refrigerate. Then slide foil on cookie sheet for baking.)
2. Dust pattern pieces with flour and arrange on dough, leaving ½-inch space between each piece.
3. With sharp, pointed paring knife, carefully cut out pieces. Carefully remove pattern pieces and all excess dough (reserve excess dough to reroll for additional cookies).
4. Bake at 400°F for 8 to 10 minutes, or until edges are lightly browned. Cool completely before removing from foil.
5. To make logs, roll reserved excess dough into 2 ropes ⅜-inch thick by 10-in. long. Cut into 2-inch lengths. Place on foiled-lined cookie sheet. Bake at 400°F for 8 to 10 minutes, or until lightly browned. Cool completely before removing from foil.

Frosting the pieces

1. Frost the figures and barn as illustrated on the previous pages or use your own imagination liberally. TIP: With a small, plain tip of a decorator pastry bag, apply white frosting to outline areas. Then with a thinner mixture and using a small paintbrush, fill in areas with colored frostings.
2. Let dry completely before assembling.

Making the base

Cover 20 × 24-inch heavy cardboard with foil. Frost entire surface with white frosting, making rough texture to resemble snow.

Assembling the farm scene

1. Begin with the barn. Spread frosting on the bottom edge of the back and bottom edge of one side; stand them together in place on the base. Fill the inside seam with frosting and let harden.
2. Finish the walls by joining the front and other side in place in the same manner.
3. Spread frosting on upper edge of back wall and rear side wall pieces; spread frosting on bottom side of roof piece where it will touch walls; put roof piece in place on walls and let dry. Repeat with other roof piece.
4. Set doors and shutters in place one by one, using frosting along seam where they meet barn.
5. Set up woodshed and fence in similar manner.
6. Arrange figures on base, setting them in place with a generous amount of frosting.

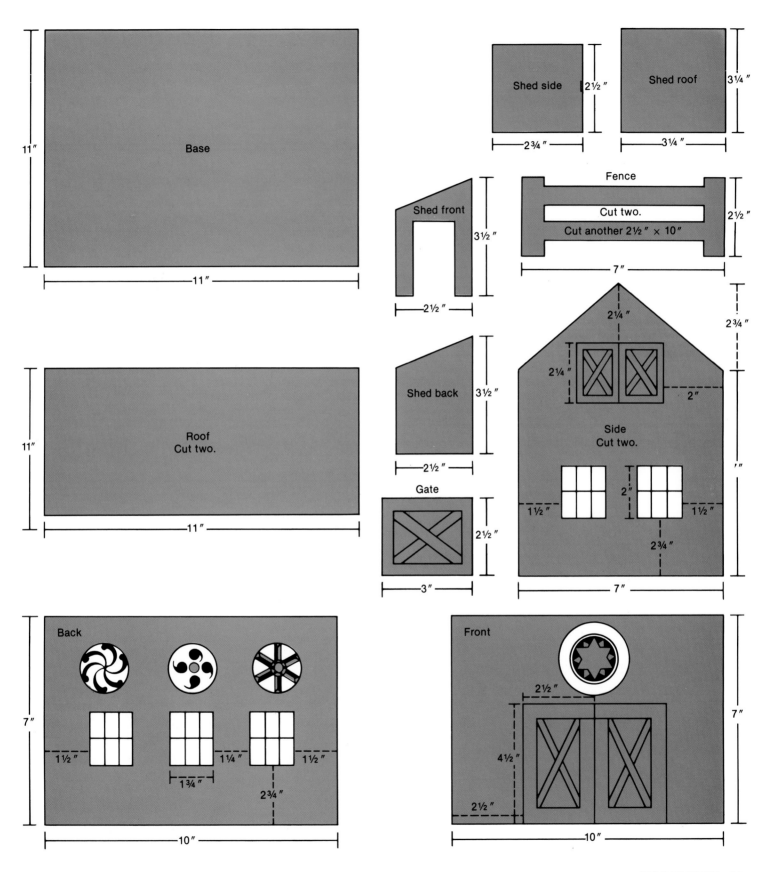

Base

11″

11″

Shed side

2½″

2¾″

Shed roof

3¼″

3¼″

Shed front

3½″

2½″

Fence

Cut two.

Cut another 2½″ × 10″

2½″

7″

2¼″

2¾″

2¼″

2″

Shed back

3½″

2½″

Side
Cut two.

2″

1½″

1½″

2¾″

7″

7″

Roof
Cut two.

11″

11″

Gate

2½″

3″

Back

7″

1½″

1¼″

1½″

1¾″

2¾″

Front

2½″

4½″

7″

2½″

10″

10″

❄ Wrapping Apron and Spoon Doll

You probably already have most of the materials needed to make this colorful carry-all apron, so why not try your hand at it? Any gift wrapper will appreciate it, not only during the holidays but all year round. The handy pockets tote everything from Christmas and greeting cards to tape, twine, scissors, and anything else needed to gift wrap presents. When you've finished, try another easy gift for a doll lover—the spoon doll, who wears her own miniature wrapping apron.

Materials for the apron

1 yd. of cotton fabric.
1½ yds. of ribbon, 1'' wide
6 yds. of trim or 6 yds. each of lace and ribbon.
Scissors, pins, needle.
Thread to match fabric.

Materials for the doll

1 wooden spoon, 14" long.
Scraps of felt: pink for hands and to match yarn.
Small amount of yarn for hair.
Milliner's wire.
Masking tape.
Felt-tip pens for face.
Piece of wood for base, 1" x 3" x 3".
Polyfill batting.
Glue.

Materials for the dress and bonnet

½ yard cotton fabric.
½ yard non-woven interfacing.
2½ yards lace.
Scissors, pins, needles.
Thread to match fabric and yarn.

After you've finished wrapping all the presents, roll up your wrapping apron with all the tools and supplies inside and tuck it away until the next session. And woe to anyone who snitches those special scissors that you use for ribbons and bows!

The origins of the spoon doll are no doubt ancient, since she has always appealed to folk artists for her simplicity: she's just a spoon. Beyond that, she can be dressed as plainly or as elaborately as your materials and skills allow. Our doll wears her own wrapping apron, an exact miniature copy of mother's full-sized apron, described in this project.

Constructing the apron

1. Make a paper pattern using the figure as a guide; pin it to the fabric and cut out, allowing a ½-in. seam all around.
2. Stitch two layers together, leaving opening to turn and press. Stitch trim in place.

Constructing the pocket for cards and pen

1. Make a pattern using the figure as a guide; pin to the fabric and cut out. Seam edges leaving an opening to turn. Clip into the corner. Turn and press.

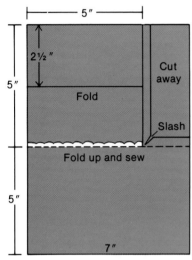

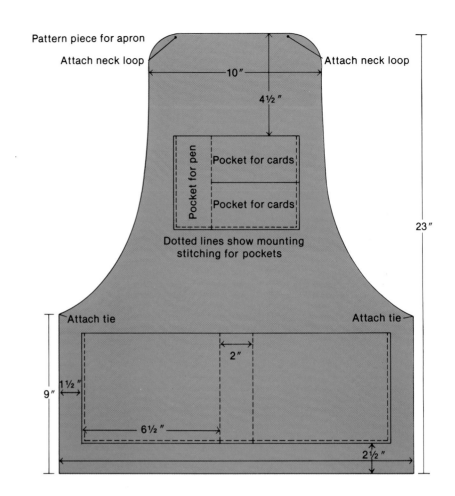

Pattern piece for apron

Attach neck loop   Attach neck loop

Dotted lines show mounting stitching for pockets

2. Fold pocket up at point indicated, forming an outer pocket. Sew on trim along pocket's upper edge.

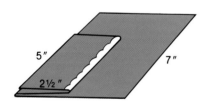

3. Sew trim around remaining areas of the pocket, as shown in figure.

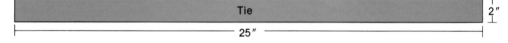

Tie

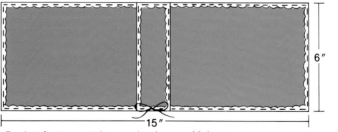

Sew trim around areas shown.

Pocket for tape, twine, and scissors. Make a bow and stitch it to the center of pocket.

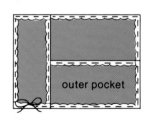

outer pocket

Pattern piece for cards-and-pen pocket.

Constructing the pocket for tape, twine, and scissors

1. Cut fabric, then seam edges, leaving opening to turn. Turn and press.
2. Sew trim over stitching lines for center pockets.
3. Sew trim around the pocket, leaving ends for a bow at center on lower edge.

Constructing the ties and neck loop

1. Cut three pieces from the fabric, each measuring 23 in. by 4 in.
2. Fold each piece in half with the right sides together, and stitch around all except the top edge. Turn each piece right-side out.
3. Turn in the edges on the ends of two of the ties and sew to form a triangular-shaped

finished edge.
4. Iron the three pieces down flat.
5. Sew trim on neck loop.

Final assembly

Using the figure as a guide, sew on the ties, neck loop, pockets, small bows, and length of ribbon for scissors.

Constructing the doll

1. Glue felt over the concave bowl of a spoon to form the back of the head. Glue yarn to the top sides of the spoon and over the felt. Turn up ends of yarn at the back to make a bun at the bottom of the bowl.

2. Draw the doll's face on the convex side of the spoon; use the photograph as a guide, or create your own features.

3. Cut two lengths of milliner's wire 10'' long and wrap them around the spoon 1'' below the bowl; secure the wire to the spoon with masking tape. Fold back the wire ends in loops to make hands. The hands should extend about 3'' from the body.

4. Cut hand shapes from pink felt, using drawing as guide. Stitch around curved edge, leaving straight edge open. Slip hands over wire loops and stitch in place.

5. To make a base for the doll, drill a hole in the center of the wood square to fit the spoon handle; glue handle in hole.

Making the dress and bonnet

1. Make patterns using the drawings as guides. Cut underskirt from non-woven interfacing; cut bodice, skirt, and hat from cotton fabric.

2. Stitch center back seam in underskirt leaving 3'' open at top.

3. Hem sleeves and neckline of bodice; sew on lace. Slash center back. Fold in half and sew underarm seams. Trim close and turn under top edge of skirt ½''; stitch close to edge.

4. Stitch back seam of skirt, leaving 2½'' open at the top. Turn hem under and press; stitch close to edge. Stitch lace over edge.

5. For the bonnet, turn under the hem and stitch close to edge. Trim away excess. Lay lace over raw edge and stitch in place. Put a gathering stitch on the line shown in the drawing and pull up to form the crown. Stuff crown with polyfill.

Attaching the dress and bonnet to doll

1. Wrap polyfill around torso and wire arms of doll. Pull bodice on and adjust amount of stuffing. Fold one edge of center back under and sew it by hand to the other side of the center back to make a seam. Sew hem of sleeve through the felt hand.

2. Gather the top of the underskirt. Stitch it to the bodice just below the waistline, as shown in the drawing.

3. Gather the skirt close to the edge by hand and stitch it to the bodice on the waistline as shown in the drawing.

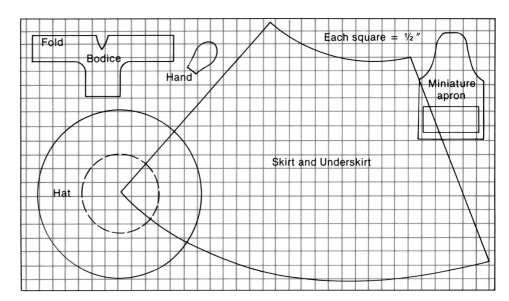

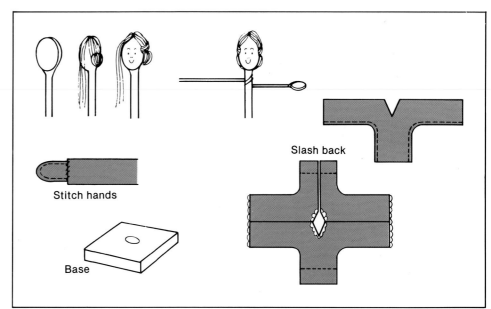

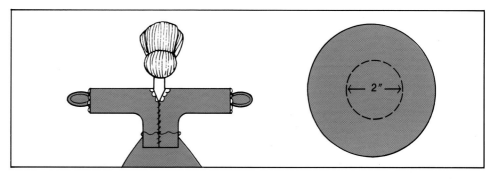

4. Put the bonnet on the doll's head and stitch it to the yarn hair with stitches placed along the gathering thread.

5. If you wish, make a miniature wrapping apron for the doll. Ours is just ⅛ the size of the one shown opposite.

Wrappings

Nothing dresses up a gift like a big bow of bright ribbon. There's a knack to making loops that hold their shape: just add a little practice to the instructions given here and you'll soon acquire it.

Materials

1½'' ribbon (number 9) for each bow. (Use 2'' ribbon for bows on larger packages or wreathes.)
23-gauge wire. (Florists carry plastic-covered and cloth-covered wire. Hardware stores carry plain wire.)
Colorful pipe cleaners.

Making a Fluffy Bow

1. Use 1½ yards of 1½'' ribbon. Hold a 3''-4'' tail between thumb and first finger. Wrap about 18'' of wire twice around the ribbon tightly, just above your fingers, leaving a 3''-4'' tail extending out of the way.

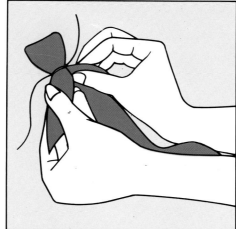

2. Make the first loop behind, about 2½'' long, pointing up. Twist the long end of the wire around the loop and pull it tight.

3. Make the second loop the same size, behind the first, but slightly to the side. Continue making loops, all pointing up, all cinched tight with a twist of wire at the center, and all to one side of the previous loop, to make a complete bow. There should be a minimum of 7 loops.

4. Cut the end of the ribbon. Arrange the loops evenly in a circle. Twist the ends of the wire together to make a 3''-4'' extension, and snip off the excess.

A Variation: the Double-Fluffy Bow

1. Use 1½ yards of both 1½'' and ½'' ribbon. Place the narrower ribbon on top of the wider in the center and cinch them together with a couple turns of wire, leaving a 3'' tail of ribbon and a 3'' extension of wire.
2. Make the loops in the same way as the fluffy bow, always pointing up and behind the previous loop. Make at least 7 loops to finish the bow.
3. The trick is to hold the two ribbons at once, keeping the narrow one in the center and making the loops the same size.

Handsome wrappings topped by beautiful bows transform a mere package into a presentation. These bows are durable enough to be saved for another gift wrapping or used as a tree ornament.

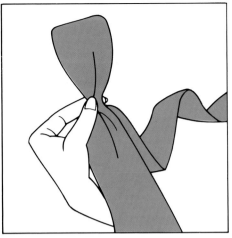

Making a Flat Bow

1. Start with 1½ yards of ribbon. Hold a 3''-4'' tail between thumb and finger.

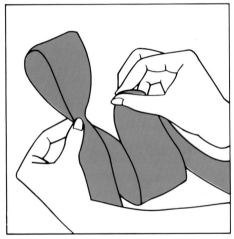

2. Make the first loop behind, about 3'' long, pointing up. Pinch the loop and grasp it with thumb and finger.

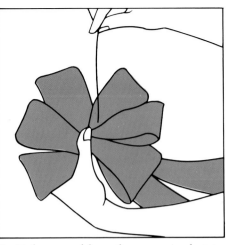

3. Make second loop the same size but to the front and pointing down. Make third loop behind the first, pointing up and to the side. Alternate several loops up and down, grasping each tightly until bow is complete.

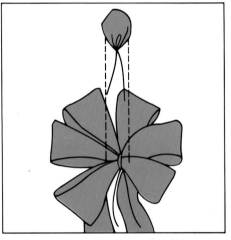

4. With all the loops gathered tightly, wrap a 6''-piece of wire or a pipe cleaner around all the loops and make two tight turns. Arrange the loops evenly in a circle.

5. Add a center knot made with a 3'' piece of ribbon; make a single loop and cinch it tight at the bottom with a short piece of wire. Clip off excess ribbon. Then insert a 6'' piece of wire through the loop, make 2 twists, and place the loop in the center of the bow with the two short pieces of wire extending through the center of the bow. Twist these wire ends together with the pipe cleaner ends and use all these wires to attach the bow to a package.

A Variation: the Wreath Bow

1. To make a bow for a wreath 18''-36'' in diameter, use about 2½-3 yards of 2½'' ribbon (number 40).

2. Make the bow just like the flat bow, but start with a 16'' tail and make the loops about 5'' long. Alternate the loops up and down, making a minimum of 6 loops. Wrap a pipe cleaner tightly around all the loops. Make a center knot from a 6'' piece of ribbon in the same way as for the flat bow. Cut the final tail to match the first.

Hints for Pretty Bows

1. If you are right-handed, hold loops in the left hand and feed with the right. If you are left-handed, hold loops with the right hand and feed with the left.
2. Don't make loops too large: with 1½'' ribbon, 3'' loops are about right.
3. Make all loops the same size.
4. Avoid creasing the loops. To adjust the loops while making, insert two fingers inside the loop and expand gently.
5. When carrying, shipping, or storing bows, put tissue paper or other soft material inside the loops to prevent creasing.

Topic Wrapping

Here's an idea for an unusual gift wrapping: Dress the package to suggest what's inside. To wrap a blouse, for example, cover the box with colorful fabric (you probably have just the right thing among your remnants) and then add bits of ribbon and buttons to represent the placket front. Another bit of ribbon suggests the collar line. Other possibilities: for a necktie, cut a piece of flamboyant fabric in tie-shape and glue it to a contrasting background in solid color; for a pair of gloves, cut a pair of glove shapes from imitation leather, or fabric, or knitted material (whip the edges) and attach them to the box, along with a key ring and a few keys cut out of gold and silver paper.

Christmas Stockings

The tradition of stuffing stockings or shoes with fruits, sweets, and small toys is as old as Saint Nicholas himself. It is especially fun to make and give one of these colorful stockings because you know that it will be used and loved year after year.

"The stockings were hung by the chimney with care." And now that St. Nicholas has filled them with goodies, and whisked back up the chimney, they hang ready for the children, whose joyous cries will soon fill the house.

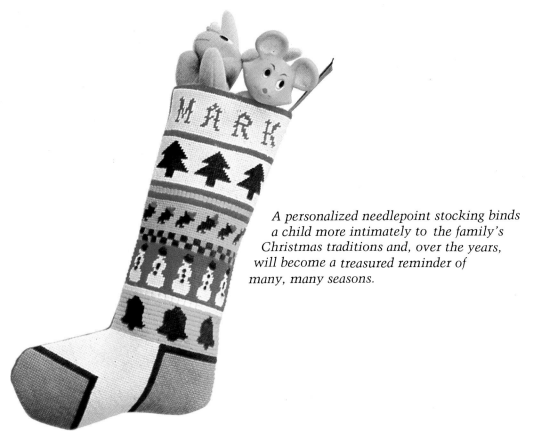

A personalized needlepoint stocking binds a child more intimately to the family's Christmas traditions and, over the years, will become a treasured reminder of many, many seasons.

Materials and supplies

General: 2 to 4 pieces of fabric or felt, 10" x 17"; seam tape, braid or ribbon (for hanging loop); alphabet stencil with ½" capital letters (for personalized stockings); dressmakers' carbon paper.

Applique and embroidery: 6-ply cotton embroidery floss in appropriate colors; felt in various colors for cutting out design or letter shapes; sewing needle and thread.

Needlepoint: 21" x 12" square of quality mono canvas, no larger than No. 12 gauge; enough material or felt for 2 extra stocking shapes with which to make a stocking liner; needlepoint yarn and needle. The amount and size of yarn you use will vary depending upon the size canvas you purchase and the needlepoint stitch you choose. You should check with your local needlework shop and buy needle, yarn, and canvas at the same time, because it is difficult to match yarn dye lots at a later date.

Fabric painting: Artists' acrylic or fabric paint in red, blue, yellow, black and white; small, artists' quality paint brush; waxed paper. You should use a smooth-finished fabric if you plan to paint a stocking design, because any kind of a napped fabric causes the paint to spread.

Enlarging the patterns

1. Select a pattern from the gridded designs given.
2. Tape two pieces of typing paper together along the longer edges and rule off the sheet into ¹¹/₁₆-in squares.
3. Transfer the gridded stocking design of your choice to your ruled paper, one square at a time.
4. After selecting your fabric and decorating method, use dressmakers' carbon paper to transfer your full-sized pattern to the fabric.

Applique or embroidery

1. Transfer an enlarged pattern to the fabric or felt.
2. Cut out the pattern pieces and sew them to a stocking shape by using a blind stitch around the edges (use two or three plies of 6-ply cotton embroidery thread for all stitches).

For example, to applique the snowman, you could trace the stocking shape onto red felt and the snowman shape onto white felt. Then cut out and attach the snowman using a blind stitch.

3. Apply the details by embroidering or cutting them out of felt and then stitching them in place.

4. Personalize the stocking by appliqueing stenciled letters cut from felt or fabric, or embroidering letters stenciled directly onto the stocking top.

Fabric painting

1. Transfer an enlarged design to a smooth finished material.
2. Place waxed paper under fabric.
3. Paint on the background first, then the details, applying an extra coat if you are using a light color on a dark fabric. If you mix a color, be sure to mix enough to complete the portion you are painting, as it is very difficult to remix and exactly match colors.
4. Personalize by stenciling a name or monogram on the stocking top and then painting in the letters.

Needlepoint

1. The entire stocking-front design and background can be executed in the Basketweave or Continental stitch (Skills Pages). Both stitches give the same front appearance. The Basketweave stitch requires more yarn to complete the project, but has the advantage of distorting the canvas very little, making the finished project easier to press back into shape.
2. Personalize the stocking by using letters from the supplied needlepoint alphabet (Skills Pages). Center the name or monogram at the top of the stocking.

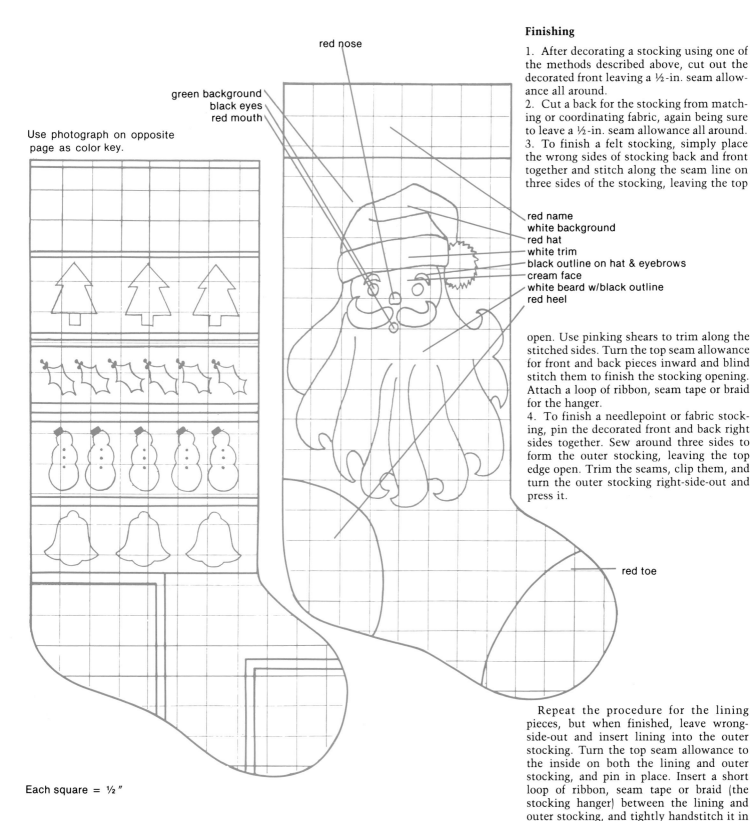

red nose

green background
black eyes
red mouth

Use photograph on opposite page as color key.

Each square = ½″

red name
white background
red hat
white trim
black outline on hat & eyebrows
cream face
white beard w/black outline
red heel

red toe

Finishing

1. After decorating a stocking using one of the methods described above, cut out the decorated front leaving a ½-in. seam allowance all around.

2. Cut a back for the stocking from matching or coordinating fabric, again being sure to leave a ½-in. seam allowance all around.

3. To finish a felt stocking, simply place the wrong sides of stocking back and front together and stitch along the seam line on three sides of the stocking, leaving the top open. Use pinking shears to trim along the stitched sides. Turn the top seam allowance for front and back pieces inward and blind stitch them to finish the stocking opening. Attach a loop of ribbon, seam tape or braid for the hanger.

4. To finish a needlepoint or fabric stocking, pin the decorated front and back right sides together. Sew around three sides to form the outer stocking, leaving the top edge open. Trim the seams, clip them, and turn the outer stocking right-side-out and press it.

Repeat the procedure for the lining pieces, but when finished, leave wrong-side-out and insert lining into the outer stocking. Turn the top seam allowance to the inside on both the lining and outer stocking, and pin in place. Insert a short loop of ribbon, seam tape or braid (the stocking hanger) between the lining and outer stocking, and tightly handstitch it in place. Whipstitch the lining to the outer stocking around the top.

Chapter 2: The Tree

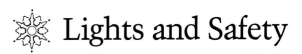

Checking the Christmas Tree Lights

1. Spread the string of lights out on the floor or sofa. Tighten all of the bulbs in their sockets, then plug in the string.
2. Replace any bulbs that have burned out. (Be aware that some European-style light strings have bulbs which cannot be removed.)

Untangling Christmas tree lights every year

can be a real threat to the Yuletide spirit. A good way to prevent tangled lights is to wind them around an empty paper towel tube and tape down the loose end.

If none of the bulbs light,

the string may be series-type, which will not light unless every bulb is working. You can test the bulbs by using one of these methods:

1. Look at each bulb under a strong light to see if the filament (the thin wire that glows when the bulb is lit) is broken; if it is, the bulb won't work.
2. Using a continuity tester (inexpensively purchased at most hardware or radio and electronics stores), touch its alligator clip to one contact point and the probe end to the other end on each bulb. If the tester lamp lights, the bulb is good.
3. Use a 9-volt transistor radio battery as a tester by touching the bulb contact points to the battery terminals. If the bulb glows, it works.

If every bulb is working but the string still does not light,

you can check if one or more of the sockets has disconnected wires that need to be resoldered. Using a continuity tester and soldering gun or iron, follow these steps:
1. Unplug the string and fasten the alligator clip of the tester across both prongs of the plug.
2. Starting with the bulb socket closest to the plug, touch the center and the threaded side of the socket simultaneously with the probe end of the tester. If the tester lamp lights, the socket is wired correctly.
3. Put a bulb that works into the tested socket, and repeat the process for the next socket away from the plug end of the string. Continue the process, putting a working bulb into each tested socket that works.
4. When you find a socket that does not light the tester's lamp, carefully remove and resolder both wires to their connection points on the base. In order to avoid shock, it may be necessary to use high quality plastic electrician's tape to cover resoldered connections.
5. If the socket passes the test, continue until all sockets in the string have been tested.
6. If the socket fails the test even after the connections have been re-soldered (or if the design of the socket has made re-soldering impossible), then remove the bad socket by cutting the wires on both sides of it. Next, strip, splice, solder, and tape the wire ends back together and continue testing.

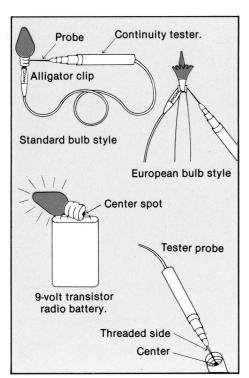

The warm glow of Christmas lights signals that special season when friendship and family ties gladden hearts in every home.

✳ Evergreen Guide

Red Pine.   *Although native only to the eastern half of North America, this straight, fast growing tree is also known as the Norway pine. It is easy to recognize by its reddish-brown bark and paired needles that grow in tufts near the ends of the branches. A northern tree, the red pine is cultivated widely in tree plantations from the Great Lakes region to New England.*

Until relatively recent times, the tree decorating most people's homes during the holidays would have been the fir. Some have traced this ancient tradition as far back as 18th-century Germany. There are other species, though, that have now become popular choices along with the fir. Here are six of them that are Christmas-time favorites. Which do you prefer? Remember one characteristic that they *all* have in common: conveying the message of peace and good will by the simplest of all means—bringing the timeless fragrance of the forest into your home.

Black Spruce.   *If you prefer a small, tabletop tree, chances are it will be a black spruce. These slender, slow-growing trees, thriving in the sphagnum bogs of the far north, are utilized completely. Their wood is a main source of Canada's paper pulp, their resin is used for chewing gum, and even the tips of their branches once had a purpose—for making spruce beer.*

Scotch Pine.   *This tree is not a native of the United States, but of Europe and northern Asia. It grows abundantly in forested areas across northern Europe, including Russia. The Scotch pine has been extensively planted in the United States, since it grows well in dry, infertile soil. Under plantation conditions, it grows fast and becomes bushy when pruned and sheared. Thus, most Scotch pine Christmas trees are plantation-grown.*

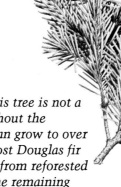

Douglas Fir.   *In spite of its name and appearance, this tree is not a fir but belongs in a genus of its own and is found throughout the western United States, on both sides of the Rockies. It can grow to over 300 feet tall, and may live to be over 1,000 years old. Most Douglas fir Christmas trees are young ones that have been removed from reforested areas. Their removal helps to thin the forest, allowing the remaining trees to grow faster.*

Balsam Fir.   *The symmetrical shape, fragrance, rich green color, and ability of its needles to remain vital and firmly attached long after the tree has dried out—these characteristics have made the balsam fir the prototype of Christmas trees. Found over a wide area of the eastern United States and Canada, it averages 25 to 60 feet in height; however, a dwarf form of the tree is common at elevations of approximately 5,000 feet.*

Eastern Red Cedar.   *This tree grows from the Atlantic coast to central Kansas and Nebraska. It will grow in almost any kind of soil, but may never become anything more than a bush in some of the poor soil regions of the north. Under better conditions, it can reach 100 feet in height. The eastern red cedar is more accurately referred to as a juniper, since there are no true cedars on this continent.*

Ornaments

A pine tree, all but hidden under a cloud of old-fashioned ornaments, was the focal point of Victorian homes at Christmas time. Many of the hand-made decorations have been in the family for generations. Each one recalls holiday memories.

Calico Patches

A few scraps of leftover fabric, a bit of stuffing, plus a few quick stitches—and you have charming and colorful decorations in miniature. These calico patches make soft highlights for the tree, the mantel, or a table decoration, and they add an old-fashioned accent to a Christmas stocking or a special gift wrapping.

Although the three little kittens cuddling in the basket are more than one-hundred years old, they reflect the ageless quality of true folk art. Made of calico patches, with a minimum of detail and only a bit of string around their necks, they were not meant to be realistic. But to the child who treasured them they were the very essence of kitten.

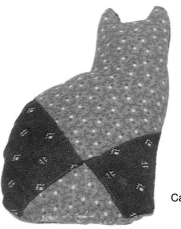

Cat

Pillow

Materials

Fabric scraps.
Buttons.
Lace trim.
Polyfill stuffing.

Making the decorations

1. Cut and sew fabric scraps together into larger pieces.
2. Cut out two identical pieces of fabric, one from patchwork and one from solid color, using the photographs (or your imagination) as guides for the shape.
3. With the right sides together, stitch contrasting pairs of fabric together, leaving a small opening at one end. Clip and trim seam allowance.
4. Turn right-side out and stuff with polyfill. Slipstitch opening closed.
5. Tack trim and buttons onto pillows. Sew a small loop of trim at the center balance point of each, for hanging from the tree.

Dove

Heart

Crocheted Ornaments

Here are three suggestions for Christmas-tree ornaments that anyone with basic crocheting skills can make. And like real snowflakes, the geometry of these can be varied in myriad ways, or the bauble decorated as your repertoire of stitches and your imagination permit. The finished ornaments can be stiffened with acrylic spray, but the old-fashioned country way is to dip them in a thick sugar solution and let them dry.

Christmas Ball (Left)

Materials

1 ball White Size 30 Clark's Crochet Cotton; Size 8 steel crochet hook; 2 yds. ⅛"-wide green satin ribbon; two tiny pinecones and sprigs of holly berries; two round balloons.

To make

Ch 25; join with sl st to form ring.
Round 1: Ch 6, dc in ring; *ch 1, dc in ring. Rep from * 16 times, end ch 1, sl st in ch-6 sp at beg of rnd.
Round 2: Ch 7, dc in ch-6 of prev rnd; *ch 2, dc in next sp. Rep from * around, end ch 2, sl st in ch-7 sp at beg of rnd.
Round 3: Ch 8, trc in ch-7 sp of prev rnd; *ch 3, trc in next sp. Rep from * around, end ch 3, sl st in ch-8 sp.
Round 4: Ch 9, d trc (wind thread 3 times around hook) in ch-8 sp; *ch 4, d trc in next sp. Rep from * around, end ch 4, sl st in ch-9 sp.
Round 5: Rep Round 4, fasten off.
Make second piece the same. Dissolve 1 cup sugar in ½ cup water. Bring to boil. Blow up balloons to 10" diameter. Dip each crocheted piece in sugar solution. Place one piece on each balloon, molding to fit. Let dry on balloons overnight. When thoroughly dry, remove carefully from balloons. Tie the two parts together with ribbon bows. Tie holly to bottom. Drop pinecones into ball through top opening. Tie on ribbon hanging loop.

Snowflake (Center)

1 ball White Size 50 American Thread Company "Star" Crochet Cotton; Size 13 steel crochet hook.

To make

Ch 4; join with sl st to form ring.
Round 1: Ch 8, dc in ring. *Ch 5, dc in ring. Rep from * 3 times, ch 2, dc in 3rd st of ch (this brings thread in position for next round).
Round 2: Ch 3, sc over dc just made. *Ch 7, sc in next lp, ch 3, sc in same sp, rep from * 4 times, ch 3, trc in dc.
Round 3: Ch 3, sc in trc. *Ch 9, sc in 4th st from hook for picot, ch 3, sc in same sp, ch 3, sl st in same sp (picot cluster), rep from * twice, ch 5, sc in next ch-7 lp, ch 3, sc in same sp; rep from first * 4 times; *ch 9, sc in 4th st from hook for picot, ch 3, sc in same sp, ch 3, sl st in same sp, rep from * twice, ch 5, sl st in trc, cut thread.
Round 4: Attach thread in center picot of 3rd picot cluster of any lp; **ch 7, sl st in 4th st from hook for picot, ch 7, sl st in 4th st from hook for picot, *ch 4, sl st in 4th st from hook for picot, rep from * once, *ch 3, sl st in same sp, rep from last * twice, working on other side, *sl st in same space with next picot, ch 3, sl st in same sp, rep from * once, ch 7, sl st in 4th st from hook for picot, ch 3, sc in center picot of next picot cluster, ch 7, sc in center picot of next picot cluster, ch 3, sc in same sp, ch 7, sc in center of next picot cluster; rep from ** all around; join, cut thread.

Snowflake (Right)

Materials

1 ball White Size 50 American Thread Company "Star" Crochet Cotton; Size 13 steel crochet hook.

To make

Round 1: *Ch 5; keeping last lp of each trc on hook, work 3 trc in 4th st from hook, yo and pull through all lps (rice st); rep from * 5 times. Be careful not to twist sts, join with sl st to form ring.
Round 2: Ch 4; keeping last lp of each trc on hook, work 2 trc in same sp, yo and pull through all lps, ch 4, sl st in same sp with joining petal, ch 4; keeping last lp of each trc on hook, 3 trc in same sp with joining, yo and through all lps; *ch 3; keeping last lp of each trc on hook, work 3 trc in ch-1 between next 2 rice sts, yo and through all lps, ch 4, sl st in same ch-1, ch 4; keeping last lp of each trc on hook, work 3 trc in same ch-1, yo and through all lps; rep from * around; ch 3, join in top of first petal.
Round 3: Work 3 rice sts same as on Round 1; sl st in top of next petal, ch 3, sl st in top of next petal. Rep from beg around. Cut thread.
Round 4: Attach thread in the ch-1 bet first 2 rice sts; **ch 5, sl st in 4th st from hook for picot, *ch 5, sl st in 4th st from hook for picot; rep from * twice, ch 1, sc in the ch-1 bet next 2 rice sts; ch 7, sl st in 4th st from hook for picot; *ch 5, sl st in 4th st from hook for picot; rep from last * 4 times; dc in the ch-1 bet 3rd and 4th picots from hook, ch 5, sl st in 4th st from hook for picot, trc bet next 2 picots on opposite side, ch 5, sl st in 4th st from hook for picot, d trc (3 times over hook) bet next 2 picots on opposite side, ch 5, sl st in 4th st from hook for picot; skip 1 picot, tr trc (4 times over hook) in next st of ch on opposite side, ch 2, skip 1 rice st and ch-3 lp, sc in ch bet next 2 rice sts; rep from ** around; join, cut thread.

How to stiffen snowflake ornaments

Dissolve 1 cup sugar in ½ cup water. Bring to boil. Immerse crocheted piece in this solution until thoroughly saturated. With tongs, remove and place on paper towel. Cover a piece of cardboard with waxed paper. With rustproof pins, pin the wet crocheted piece to shape on cardboard. Let dry overnight.

The infinite variety and fine detail of real snowflakes inspired the intricate stitches of these delicate, crocheted snowflake ornaments.

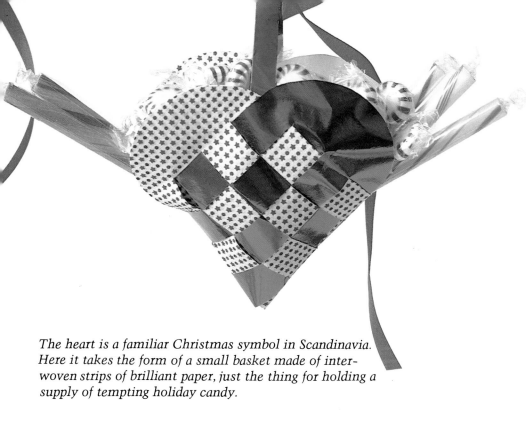

Woven Hearts

All you need to make these festive ornaments from the Scandinavian Christmas tradition is brightly colored paper, some ribbon, and, of course, plenty of candies or gifts to fill them before hanging them on the tree. Children will find that weaving the pieces together makes a delightful puzzle to solve.

The heart is a familiar Christmas symbol in Scandinavia. Here it takes the form of a small basket made of interwoven strips of brilliant paper, just the thing for holding a supply of tempting holiday candy.

Materials for each heart

One piece of stiff paper, cloth, or felt, measuring at least 8½'' x 11''.
Ribbon, cloth, felt, or paper strip measuring approximately 6'' long, for the handle.
Thread and needle or glue for attaching handle to basket.
Small candies or gifts.

Cutting and weaving instructions

1. Fold the piece of cloth or paper in half. Cut out two identical shapes, using the dimensions shown.
2. Insert Strip 1 into Strip A. Then open Strip 1 and insert Strip B. Open Strip C and insert Strip 1; open Strip 1 and insert Strip D. One strip will now be interwoven.
3. Slide the interwoven strip up about ¾-in. on the other piece of paper, and begin interweaving Strip 2, making sure to alternate the weave (i.e., begin by opening Strip 2 and inserting Strip A, etc.).
4. Repeat Steps 2 and 3 for the remaining strips. The result: a heart-shaped woven basket.
5. Fold the strip of paper or cloth to form a handle. Staple, sew, or glue it to the inside of the basket. Now you're ready to fill the basket with candies or small gifts and hang from the Christmas tree.

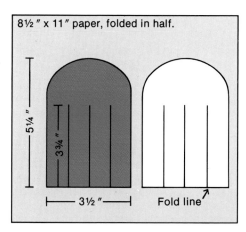

8½'' x 11'' paper, folded in half.

5¼''

3¾''

3½''

Fold line

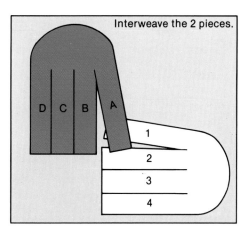

Interweave the 2 pieces.

D C B A

1
2
3
4

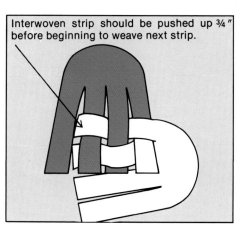

Interwoven strip should be pushed up ¾'' before beginning to weave next strip.

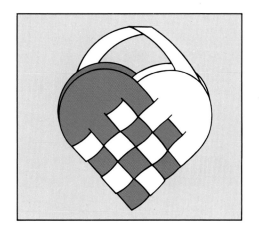

Little Fingers

Perhaps you'll want to give "little fingers" a little guidance for these projects, but the main thing is to let them join in building your family's Christmas traditions.

Gingerbread People

Here's a project for grownups and children to do together. After you've baked the gingerbread cookies, decorate them to represent people you know—family, friends, acquaintances: a short name or a simple symbol will do very nicely.

¾ cup soft vegetable shortening
1 cup firmly packed light brown sugar
¼ cup dark molasses
1 egg
2¼ cups sifted all-purpose flour
2 teaspoons baking soda
¼ teaspoon salt
½ teaspoon cloves
1 teaspoon cinnamon
1 teaspoon ginger
½ teaspoon allspice
½ teaspoon nutmeg
Confectioners' sugar for rolling out the cookies.

1. Measure the shortening, brown sugar, molasses, and egg into mixing bowl and cream together thoroughly.
2. In a separate bowl, sift together the flour and spices. Slowly stir it into the sugar and egg mixture. Make sure all ingredients are thoroughly combined.
3. After chilling dough in the refrigerator for several hours, roll it out on aluminum foil. Use the powdered sugar (instead of flour) to help prevent sticking as you roll it out.
4. Using a store-bought ''gingerbread-boy'' cutter, cut out the cookies. Cut out a hole in each one if you plan to hang them from a tree.
5. With the cookies still on the aluminum foil, place them on cookie sheets and bake for 10 to 12 minutes at 375 degrees. Yield: Approximately 24 people.
6. Decorate with simple white glaze of confectioners' sugar and water, mixed to a creamy consistency and applied in a thin line with a pastry tube.

Cinnamon Bows

A bundle of cinnamon sticks, bound with a length of colorful ribbon, makes a fragrant decoration for the holiday season.

Materials

Cinnamon sticks, as many as you like
Ribbon
Small baskets or other containers, if desired

1. Gather small bunches of sticks, fasten them with long strands of ribbon, and attach them to the boughs of your Christmas tree with generous bows fashioned of the same ribbon. Attach the bows close enough to the trunk that the branches don't droop.
2. Larger bunches of cinnamon sticks can be placed in baskets, piled on the mantel like a stack of logs, clustered like a corn shock, or included in the centerpiece of a festive table.

Mariners once risked their lives and their ships to bring the aromatic bark of the cinnamon tree back to spice-hungry Europe from its native Ceylon. Cinnamon remains a popular flavoring in holiday recipes—from cookies to mulled wine.

The Indians of British Columbia have long fashioned Canadian goose decoys of bundles of twigs bound with vines or hide thongs. This modern example is bound with brown twine, but still exhibits the natural shape and turn of the bird's head, which only an artist who has keenly observed his model in real life can capture.

Clothespins

A few dabs of paint or a few left-over findings transform a common clothespin into a key ring that's hard to lose or a tiny soldier in parade uniform to adorn your tree. Make a whole regiment of these guards to march in stiff formation across your mantle, or decorate a small table-tree with clothespin soldiers and put it in your sleeping child's bedroom on the night before Christmas.

The clothespin key ring goes together in three easy steps: attach the screw eye, slip the ring through it, and add your keys. Decorate as your fancy dictates.

Old-fashioned wooden clothespins can still be found at the five-and-ten store and, along with hanging out the wash, they're great for making something that's simple and pretty. Just paint on a design, such as the floral one pictured here, and seal it with a coat of polyurethane.

Key ring materials and tools

1 old-fashioned wooden clothespin.
1 ¾'' screw eye.
1 spring-clip key ring.
Paint in luminescent colors.
Clear polyurethane.
Cardboard box flaps.
Drill, with ³⁄₃₂'' bit.

Procedure for key ring

1. Drill a ³⁄₃₂-in. guide hole ¾-in. deep into the center of the clothespin head; insert screw eye.
2. To make painting easier, clip the clothespin onto the box flaps.
3. Paint the desired design onto the clothespin using luminescent colors.
4. When paint is dry, coat the entire clothespin with polyurethane.
5. When polyurethane is dry, clip the key ring into the screw eye.

Toy soldier materials

Clothespin.
Acrylic paint in red, black, and blue.
Gold rick-rack or similar trimming.
Scraps of white felt or suede.
Gold decorative string.
Red pom-poms, 1'' diameter (from curtains or bedspread edging).
White glue or household cement.
Small paint brushes.
Sewing needle.

Decorating the soldier

1. Paint soldier's legs in red, the waist-to-neck area in blue; leave head unpainted. Allow paint to dry thoroughly while continuing with Steps 2 and 3.
2. Cut the white fabric into strips ¼-in. wide; allow an 8-in. strip for each soldier.
3. Use a needle to thread a 6-in. length of gold string through each pom-pom, then tie the ends to form a 3-in. hanging loop.
4. Glue pom-poms to tops of clothespins.
5. Glue white strips of fabric down the outer legs of each soldier's trousers.
6. Glue a white strip on soldier, starting behind the neck and crossing around the chest with the ends meeting the tops of the trousers' side stripes.
7. Glue on a white strip for the waist band, covering the ends of the other stripes.
8. Glue on a short piece of gold trimming for the belt buckle.
9. Paint soldier's face, using black for the eyes, and red for the nose, cheeks, and mouth.

Pinecone Ornaments

A handful of small cones and a little imagination are all you need to make Christmas-tree decorations with a country look that will last indefinitely. Since pinecones are notorious dust catchers, seal these ornaments in a bag when you put them away after the holidays.

The mouse (left)—and the turkey inspecting him closely with a corn-kernel eye—are simply pinecones that have been imaginatively transformed with a few bits of felt and ribbon.

A piece of dark cardboard forms an invisible foundation for ornaments made from miniature cones. Create your own shapes: animals, bells, snowflakes, perhaps even a pinecone Santa with a cotton beard and cap.

Materials

Pinecones.
Poster board for foundations.
Glue.
Clear acrylic spray.
Trim for animals.

Directions

1. To make the wreath, star and candy cane, draw the pattern on a piece of dark poster-weight cardboard and cut it out. Glue small hemlock and larch cones in a regular pattern on both sides of the cardboard. Spray with clear acrylic. Glue a small paperclip at one point for a hanger.
2. To make animals, carefully select pinecones that suggest some characteristic of the animal you wish to make. Trim the main cone with smaller cones, acorns, corn kernels, feathers, berries, or pine needles. Pipe cleaners, wire, twigs, or branches can be used for legs. Attach a bit of ribbon for a hanger.

Popcorn and Cranberry Swags

There's no homier a decoration for the tree than strands of popcorn and cranberries. Glass and plastic baubles come and go, but these swags always add a familiar, down-home look.

Popcorn strings drape along the lower boughs settling as lightly as snow on the needles. Samantha the cat threatens nocturnal nibblers.

Materials

Popcorn (about 4 quarts of popped corn for 8 yards of strands).
Oil.
Cranberries. Use fresh, firm ones; they'll string easier and last longer. Save the mushy ones for sauce.
Heavy thread and needle.

Directions

1. If you pop the corn the usual way—crispy, for eating—many of the kernels will break when you try to string them. So keep the lid on the pan to hold the steam in and the kernels will come out soggy and tough—just right for threading. You won't be tempted to eat them, either.
2. Work with yard-long pieces of thread; the kernels tend to break if they have farther to travel. Start with a double knot at one end; thread the cranberries lengthwise and the corn any way you can.
3. Here's the creative part: decide what pattern of berries and kernels you want. You can make all-berry strands, but they're very heavy. A ratio of two or three kernels to one berry makes a nice mix. Be sure to leave enough thread at the end of the strand to join it to the next one.

Candy Poppers

If you dress Christmas candies up in colorful wrappings and ribbons, they'll make bright tree decorations—until someone realizes that the goodies inside are for eating.

Materials for each popper

1 piece of stiff paper, 8½ " × 11".
Length of ribbon, about 1' long.
Candies.
Scissors.

Directions

1. On the 8½ "-in. sides of the paper, cut 2-in. deep slashes, each slash about ¼ " wide.
2. Place a handful of candies on the paper, and roll it up.
3. Tie the ribbon around one end of the popper in a knot, and then tie a knot around the other end. Make sure there's enough slack in the ribbon to allow for hanging the popper on the tree.

AMERICAN ORIGINALS

When you create a present because you take pleasure in giving a gift from the heart, Christmas becomes a truly joyful occasion. In this section you'll find a wide enough selection of projects that you shouldn't have to buy gifts for anyone this year, unless you wish to. The projects are "American Originals" because they're based on traditional folk designs and techniques—many are easy to make, some more complicated—all durable, practical objects. Most are made to last more than one generation. From the most elaborate heirloom-quality quilt to the simplest pull-toy, from the most beautifully crafted cradle to the easiest-to-make potpourri, these projects are in the country Christmas spirit: made and given with love, crafted from simple, easily obtained materials. So that the whole family can join in the fun, we've included projects for all ages and skill levels—including gifts specially designed for children to help with, or even make alone. And for all who need to brush up on their crafts skills, the Skills Pages at the end of the book give a review of the techniques required.

Paul A. Seifert: "Residence of Mr. E. R. Jones. Town Dodgeville. Wis. 1881." Watercolor and tempera, 27½" × 21½". The artist has recorded in primitive, yet completely realistic, style an archetypal American scene—winter on the farm. For generations of Americans who traveled "over the river and through the woods to Grandmother's house," this was the kind of home they knew well. And except for the horses and sleighs, it remains a beloved scene all across northern America.

Chapter 3: Folk-Art Inspirations

Contemporary Pennsylvania artist David Ellinger painted this "Christmas Dream," imagining what an Amish child's dream of Christmas might be. Since the Amish people don't wear bright colors or celebrate Christmas in a gaudy fashion, they would never be found in real life dancing amid presents around a decorated tree while a reindeer jumped over the moon.

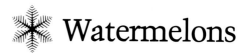

❄ Watermelons

Of all the fruits that Nature has dressed in Christmas colors, watermelons must be the most appealing. Even these braided mats and the pillow, which only look like watermelons, fairly make your mouth water for that sweet, red, summery taste. Best of all, there are no seeds to clean up after you've enjoyed them.

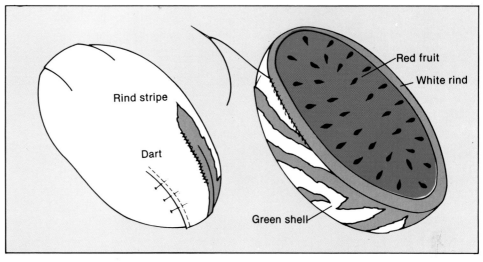

Fold and tuck the green fabric into 4 pinned darts; sew the darts. Sew the dark-green rind shapes to the shell, covering the darts.

Sew the three pieces of fabric—shell, rind, and fruit—together as explained in the instructions.

Pillow

A watermelon pillow makes a comfortable, cheerful object for a teenager to lean on.

Materials

High-density pillow or mattress foam, 5″ or 6″ thick.
Fabric: ½ yd. each of lightweight cotton in the following colors: red for the fruit; black for seeds; white for inner-rind; green for the shell; dark green for shell stripes.

Tools

Electric knife or 4″ wallpaper-stripper blade.
Large, coarse, cheese grater.
Sewing machine and supplies (thread, scissors, pins).

Cutting the foam

1. Since watermelons come in nearly every size and variation on the oval shape, you should first decide how you want yours to look. The one shown is 20 in. long and 11½ in. wide.
2. Cut the oval out of foam, beginning with the perpendicular sides.
3. Round the shell form with electric knife or wallpaper-stripper blade. When you are satisfied with the shape, smooth the knife marks away with the cheese grater.

Assembling the pillow

1. Turn the foam shape so that the rounded side is up and then pin the green fabric to it. At each end, fold and tuck the fabric into two pinned darts to make the shell fit the curved shape. (See figure.)
2. Carefully remove the shell and sew the four end-darts. Next, put the shell back onto the foam shape.
3. Cut the shapes for the rind stripes out of the dark-green fabric and pin them to the shell fabric, making sure you cover the end-dart.
4. Remove the shell from the foam and sew the shapes to the shell, using a wide, close zig-zag (buttonhole) stitch.
5. Cut the red fabric for the fruit, ¾ in. wider than the flat face of the foam shape.
6. Cut a ¾-in.-wide strip of white fabric for the inner rind. Sew it on top of the red fabric so the outer edge of the rind meets the edge of the flat oval.
7. Cut out the black seed shapes, pin them into position, and sew onto the red fabric.
8. Put the shell back onto the foam form and cut away excess material, leaving ¾ in. extra *above* the flat surface.
9. Pin the shell and fruit pieces together, folding the extra material from both inside, along the upper edge of the shell.
10. Hand stitch the shell to the outer edge of the rind.

To make a ¼-size watermelon, slice the foam form in half, lengthwise. Follow the same directions given, making only one center dart at each end of the shell form.

An unknown nineteenth-century woodsman, the story goes, noticed that the first wedge he cut out of a tree one day was shaped like a watermelon slice. So he painted it to look like a watermelon, not for any practical purpose, but like so much folk art, just for fun.

This bright, braided place mat is made exactly like a full-sized rug, but in miniature. Like the wooden watermelon slice (above), it is a whimsical interpretation of a natural object, typical of folk-art creations; nevertheless, it serves a practical function on any festive table.

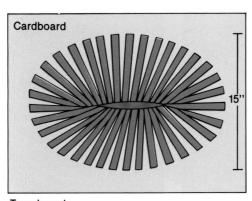

Cardboard

15"

Tape board

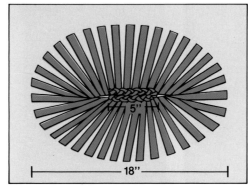

18"

Begin coiling the braid with a 5" starter length.

Place Mats

Materials to make four mats

Fabric: lightweight cotton—2 yds. each of 3 different shades of red for the fruit; ½ yd. each of 2 shades of pale-green for the rind; black scraps for the seeds.
1 roll of double-faced tape.
Cardboard piece, 15″ × 18″.

Tools

Curved needle.
Sewing machine and supplies (thread, scissors, pins).
Iron.

Constructing a mat

1. Follow the instructions on braiding (in the Skill s Pages) to make approximately 20 ft. of red braid and eight ft. of pale-green braid for each mat.
2. Lay out a tape board with the double-faced tape.
3. Begin coiling the red braid in the center of the tape board; continue until an 11-in. by 15-in. oval has been formed.
4. Add two final rows of the pale-green braid to form the rind.
5. With the braid still on the tape board, fasten the coils together with the curved needle using a long basting or tacking stitch. Begin stitching in the center and work outward.
6. Carefully remove the mat from the tape board. Set the sewing machine for a wide zigzag stitch and begin sewing the braids together, starting at the center of the mat. Continue until the entire mat is sewn together. Remember to change the machine thread from red to green when sewing the final two rows of braid.

Finishing a mat

1. Remove the tacking stitches.
2. Cut out 20 or 30 seed shapes from the black fabric scraps and pin them into position on one side of the mat.
3. Change the sewing machine stitch to a fine, medium-width zigzag and sew the seed shapes onto the mat. If you want a reversible mat, turn it over and follow the same procedure, pinning the seed shapes to the places indicated by the stitches from the other side.
4. Dampen the mat with a sponge and press it flat with a steam iron. If it will not lie flat, dampen it and place it between two towels. Put books on top and allow the mat to dry overnight .

❄ Pine Tote Box

You can use this tote box to carry eating utensils to the table, the way New Englanders did over a hundred years ago. Or, fill up its six compartments with a variety of nuts and fruits (adding some seasonal gourds for a cornucopia effect) and you have a colorful bounty to use as a centerpiece.

Materials

16'-length of ¼"-thick pine, 4" to 6" wide.
Cardboard.
Woodworking glue.
Tracing paper.
Wood stain or paint.

Tools

Protractor.
Sabre saw with fine-tooth scroll blade.
Sandpaper.
½" brads (can be substituted with careful gluing and clamping.)

Constructing and assembling the sides

1. Trace onto paper the outline of the half shapes and cut out.
2. Trace onto the lumber the outline of each full shape, twice. Write the word "inside" on each one with a pencil.
3. Draw onto tracing paper the angles shown, using a protractor, then cut out the patterns for use in setting the sabre-saw blade angles.
4. Set the sabre-saw blade at the correct angle by loosening the screw that holds the tilting base. Put the "base" edge of the paper pattern flat onto the base of the saw and tilt the base until the blade is parallel to the "blade" edge of the pattern.
5. Tighten the screw and check the angle.
6. Set the blade angle at 80°. With the "inside" of the wood surface up, cut along the slanted-end lines of all four shapes.
7. Set the blade angles at 65°. With the "inside" surface up, cut along the shorter bottom edges of all four shapes.
8. Drill ¼-in. holes through the handle-hole areas to start the sabre-saw cuts.
9. Return the saw blade to the normal setting (90°) to cut out both handle holes and the fluting on the box ends.

Knife, or utensil boxes, were common items in nineteenth-century homes. Cut out of various woods, they were often made to hang on the wall, deep enough to hold knives standing upright. The pine box shown here is a different style, since it has a handle for carrying utensils to the table. The design and somewhat thickly cut painted wood make it typical of those made in Pennsylvania. It measures 8-inches wide by 10-inches long, and the divider gives it two separate compartments. Boxes of this kind were also made with finer wood, with more compartments, frequently painted and colorfully decorated.

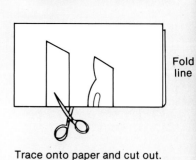

Fold line

Trace onto paper and cut out.

Shirtboard or index card

2-3″ Blade 80° Base

2-3″

2-3″ Blade 65° Base

2-3″

Draw these angles on paper and cut out to use for setting sabre-saw blade angles.

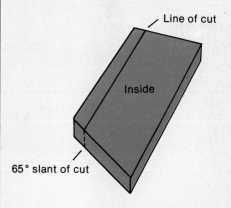

Line of cut

Inside

65° slant of cut

Set blade at 65° with "inside" face up. Cut along shorter bottom edges of all four shapes.

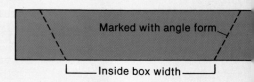

Marked with angle form

Inside box width

After checking angle of box sides with the angle form, mark the board.

Assembling the box

1. Cut out three pieces of wood which will make a 9¾-in. by 15-in. rectangle. (7)
2. With the "inside" of each side shape facing inward, test the fit of the miter cuts. To correct the angles, tack down a piece of rough sandpaper and rub the edges over it. Test and rub again until they fit. Butt the ends of the longer sides against the fluted ends. (8)
3. Apply glue to the ends of the longer sides, then butt them against the fluted ends; if you are skilled at driving brads into the end grain of thin wood, do so in order to hold the assembly in position. (Test your technique on a couple of pieces of scrap first.) If using glue only, add clamps, string, large rubber bands, weights, or any combination of these to hold the shapes in place while the glue is drying. Be sure the bottom edge of each side lies flush when the connected sides are set on a flat surface.
4. When the glue is dry at the side joints, apply glue to the bottom edges of all four sides and center them on the 9¾-in. by 15-in. box bottom. Clamp, tie, or weight the joints until the glue is dry.

Making a center divider

1. Measure the inside length, then the inside width, of the bottom of the box to find the midpoints.
2. Transfer these measurements to a piece of wood, leaving at least a 2-in. margin at each end for the angle cut. Also allow an inch or two extra in height. The excess will be taken off later.
3. Make a 62° angle form, using the protractor and some cardboard to check the

angle of the box sides at the midpoint. Adjust if necessary until the divider fits the box precisely. Then mark the board using the angle form. (9)
4. With the sabre-saw blade set at 90°, cut out the divider.
5. Insert the divider into the box at the midpoint and mark the height of the box sides.

For a fluted center divider, use the pattern shown. For a straight divider, draw a line across and cut at a 90° angle. (10)
6. Glue the divider into place at a 90° angle to the bottom of the box.

Making segment dividers

1. Measure along the box bottom from the center divider to one end. Mark this measurement on a piece of wood.
2. Check the angle on the end of the box with the angle form. Mark the angle on the wood, making the other end 90° as shown. (1)
3. Cut out two shapes like this with the sabre saw at a 90° setting. Glue the shapes into place on either side of the handle holes.
4. Repeat this procedure for the other end of the box.

Finishing

After lightly sanding and smoothing the sharp edges, the box can be painted or stained. Suggested paint colors include Williamsburg blue, bayberry green, Chinese red, or black, with Pennsylvania Dutch or Toleware-style designs added to the painted box. Possible stain choices are cherry, pine, walnut, or maple.

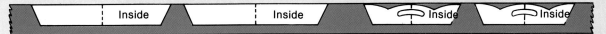

Trace outline of shapes onto lumber. Write "inside" on each shape with pencil.

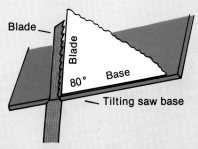

Tilt the sabre-saw blade's base until it's parallel to the "blade" edge of the paper form.

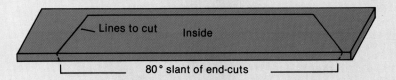

With blade angle set at 80°, and the surface marked "inside" face up, cut along slanted-end lines of all four shapes.

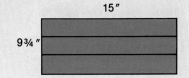

Glue pieces side to side to form box bottom.

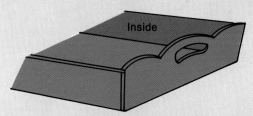

With "inside" facing inward, test the fit of the miter cuts; butt the ends of the longer sides against fluted ends.

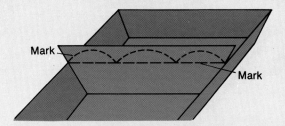

For fluted center divider, use pattern to mark as shown. For straight center divider, draw across, as indicated by dotted lines; cut at 90°.

Transfer angle to lumber and make end 90°.

"Friendship" and "Album" quilts both represent personal statements about the quilters' lives and the lives of those around them. Friendship quilts were traditionally made by a group of friends as a present for one of them. Frequently the quilts were assembled at social "bees" after each friend had pieced together a block which was usually her own or a commonly agreed-upon design; she also signed and dated it, sometimes adding a personal message. The friends then presented the assembled quilt to a bride-to-be, relative, or someone close to them to commemorate a special event. Album quilts, too, were a group effort. Sometimes all quilters worked the same design; sometimes each was assigned a different one. These usually incorporated symbols of important personal events and dates, rather than subjective statements.

Both of these traditions fit the spirit of a gift made by the members of any group — a family, a group of friends, a club or an organization — for a relative, a friend, or a retiring officer, for example. Even if a group of people share the work, making and assembling a quilt takes weeks: to piece the patches; to sew them together for the quilt's top; to border it; to sew together the "sandwich" composed of top, batting, and backing; and, finally, to sew through it with the quilting pattern of stitches. A pillow cover with five squares may be more practical than a bed cover with twenty-five.

Apparently this quilt was six years in the making as a wedding present for the new Mrs. Hittie E. Smith, born Miss Mehitabel Edwards. It was pieced together in a seacoast town north of Boston, just ten years before the War Between the States broke out. The center patches are signed with names like Cole, Wilson, Rantoul, Batchelder, Tuck, Cross, Glidden, Cleaves, Hodges, Griffin, Moses, Patterson, Wholley, Allen, Roundy — young women with old New England names. Twenty-five of her friends and relatives from the towns of Beverly, Salem, and Marblehead did the work. Some of their fathers and husbands were captains of coastal sailing ships that carried lumber to the Caribbean and came back with molasses and rum. Some of them were clipper captains in the China trade. (Rebekah Allen made a patch. Her husband was lost at sea.)

Friendship Quilt

"Mary L. Flanders. No grief can change their day to night. The darkness of that land is light." *She was the wife of the minister of the First Baptist Church in Beverly, Mass.*

"May you be free from cares and woes, When 'neath this quilt ye seek repose. Martha J. Roundy, 1849." *She later was married to William Remmonds, a sea captain.*

Clues to a quilt's age, origin, and purpose.

A multi-patterned quilt provides ample resources for an investigation into its age. The proliferation of fabrics, colors, prints, and block patterns all provide clues. Because quilts were pieced, for the most part, from fabrics that were readily accessible, methods of manufacturing, dyeing, and printing, as well as availability of raw materials (cotton, etc.) *and* fashion dictated a woman's wardrobe and, subsequently, her quilt materials. Certain browns, for example, can be traced to the second quarter of the nineteenth century when vegetable dyes were replaced by mineral dyes and a new variety of brown tones became both affordable and popular. Similarly, in the second half of the eighteenth century, copperplating replaced hand blocking (done with wooden blocks with designs cut in relief) as the most prevalent method of printing. A new variety of clearer patterns was made possible.

The quilt pictured here was made in the mid-nineteenth century. It is a "Friendship Medley" quilt, one in which each block is pieced and, in this example, signed and dated by a different friend of the owner. Then, usually, they are assembled, bordered, and quilted at a party given for that purpose. The scraps are of their own providing. The patterns, too, are often of their own choosing, though in this example the pattern remains constant.

Quilt-block patterns have many different names. To trace the quilt's origin, it would be helpful to know the names given the blocks by their makers. If the largest of the patches was called a "Ship's Wheel," it indicated that the quilters probably came from a coastal area, perhaps New England. If, on the other hand, it was called the "Prairie Star," the quilter would, of course, have come from farther inland, and the same is true of the title, "Harvest Sun." But such information is not always available. In this example, one of the signature patches reveals that it was made in Beverly, Massachusetts.

The quilt-block patterns are themselves often difficult to identify. Not only did quilters improvise and adapt designs—and, of course, not every design can be recorded — but the fabric patterns changed the *appearance* of a block. By simply making one element of the design brighter or darker than another, the same quilt block can look completely different and can take on a different name. The basic design used in the friendship quilt pictured here has many aliases, among them: "Snowflake," "Cross Stitch," "Snow Block," "The House Jack Built," and "Triple Stripe." This quilt is remarkably uniform. Only one design was used throughout; the center square was always made light, the radiating arms always darker. Still, the relatively darker or lighter fabrics chosen by the different women who worked on this quilt change the character of the squares from place to place. Imagine how different the same design would look if the elements within

the block were changed from square to square. Making the points of each cross with light-colored fabric, for example, would alter its design dramatically even though the geometry remained the same.

How to Piece, Applique and Quilt — An Overview

Decide on design and pattern, fabric and color, piecework or appliqué or a combination.

Figure out how much yardage you need for the piecework or appliqué top, the batting (middle stuffing or filling), and the backing. Get all your tools together—those for making templates, marking, and cutting fabric and those for doing the actual sewing.

Prepare the fabric—test for colorfastness, preshrink, straighten, and iron if necessary.

1. Transfer your design to graph paper and enlarge or reduce it if necessary.
2. Transfer your design to tracing paper and cut out patterns for making templates (permanent patterns to be used when cutting out fabric pieces).
3. Cut templates of cardboard, sandpaper, or posterboard.
4. Mark your fabric for cutting out the pieces for the top.
5. Cut out the fabric pieces and organize them in preparation for stitching.
6. For both piecework and appliqué, carefully baste all seams before doing the final stitching by hand or machine.
7. For piecework, stitch the individual blocks together, then join the blocks to complete the top.

OR For appliqué, stitch the pieces of the pattern onto other fabric pieces to construct the top.

8. Cut out the batting and back.
9. Select one or several patterns of quilting stitches which complement and enhance your piecework or appliqué design.
10. Mark the quilting pattern(s) on the top of the work *or* mark the quilting stitch lines after you assemble the layers.
11. Assemble the three layers of the quilting project and baste them firmly together.
12. Decide whether or not you are going to use a frame to quilt and, if so, what kind.
13. Do the final quilting, generally using a frame for large pieces, perhaps working in your lap for small ones.
14. Complete the project by finishing off the edges with binding, with pieced or appliquéd border designs, or with a self-hem of the backing fabric.

How to Clean a Quilt

The age and condition of the quilt and its fiber content will determine the type of cleaning. Start with the simplest and safest method.

Take great care with old quilts not to damage weakened fabric or batting material. Old cotton batting can lump and shift when agitated during the machine washing or drycleaning process. Tied comforters are especially prone to this problem because they don't have quilting stitches to secure the batting.

In some cases, dry cleaning is the safest process to clean a quilt. However, it does involve agitation and is hard on fragile fabrics. Consequently, gentle wet cleaning may be preferred. Unless the quilt is new and filled with fiberfill, it should be hand-washed. To wash a quilt, fold it and soak it in a bathtub filled with detergent and water for at least thirty minutes. If the water becomes dirty, repeat the process with a fresh solution. Remember, the quilt will be heavy when wet, so be sure to support it during the washing process and keep it as flat as possible. Avoid scrubbing. Agitation should be limited to an up-and-down movement with an open hand or sponge. To dry a quilt, first let it drain by placing it on a fiber-glass window screen. Next, spread it flat on a clean bed sheet, preferably outside in the shade on a breezy day. Never machine dry it or hang it on a clothesline.

New polyester and cotton fabrics and polyester fiberfill battings do not tend to lump or shift. Quilts made from these materials can often be safely machine washed and dried. Unless a quilt is noticeably soiled, airing and vacuuming may be the only cleaning it requires. In the case of fragile quilts, this may be the only technique possible. Fragile quilts can be safely vacuumed by covering them with fiberglass screening and using an upholstery tool.

A sampler of patterns for patchwork quilt squares

Legend

1. Flying Geese
   Wild Goose Chase

2. Corn and Beans
   Shoo-Fly
   Handy Andy
   Hen and Chickens
   Duck and Ducklings

3. Jacob's Ladder (New Eng.)
   Stepping Stones (New Eng. & Va.)
   The Tail of Benjamin's Kite (Miss.)
   Trail of the Covered Wagon,
      or Wagon Tracks (prairie states)
   Underground Railroad (Ky.)

4. North Carolina Lily
   Mountain Lily (Tenn., Ky.)
   Fire Lily (Oh., Ill.)
   Prairie Lily, or Noon Day
      Lily (Mid West)
   Wood Lily (New Eng.)
   Meadow LIly (Conn.)
   Mariposa Lily (Calif.)

5. Honeycomb
   Hexagon

6. Robbing Peter to Pay Paul

7. Pine Tree
   Tree of Paradise
   Christmas Tree
   Tree of Life
   Temperance Tree

8. Friendship
   Album
   Autograph

9. Log Cabin

10. Triple Irish Chain

11. Rose of Sharon

12. Sunburst

13. Hands All Around (Mid West)

14. Drunkard's Path
    Rocky Road to Dublin
    Rocky Road to California
    Country Husband
    Robbing Peter to Pay Paul
       (Salem, Oh.)

15. Coxcomb

16. Double Monkey Wrench
    Love Knot
    Hole-in-the-Barn-Door
    Puss-in-the-Corner
    Shoo-Fly
    Lincoln's Platform
    Sherman's March

17. Baby Blocks
    Tumbling Blocks
    Pandora's Box
    Stairs of Illusion
    Cube Work

18. Cherry Basket

Copper Sconce

A sheet of copper or tin and a few tools are all that's needed to create a Scandinavian sconce, a gift that anyone will appreciate any time of the year. Its simple beauty makes a handsome adornment for virtually any kind of wall, but it looks especially great hanging over a fireplace mantel.

Shiny sheet copper can easily be cut and bent to form this heart-shaped sconce. The heart itself protects the wall from heat and increases the candle's power by reflecting a warm glow into the room.

Materials

8'' x 12'' copper or tin sheet.
Tin snips.
Filing implement.
Hammer.
Small, sharp chisel or screwdriver.
Propane torch.

Instructions

1. Trace and transfer the two pattern shapes onto the tin or copper and cut them out with tin snips; file the edges.
2. Roll the candle holder cup piece until it is 1¼ in. in diameter.
3. Make a 90° bend as shown.
4. Using a propane torch, solder the cup to the base.
5. Cut out a hole at the top of the heart, using a hammer and chisel or screwdriver; file the edges.

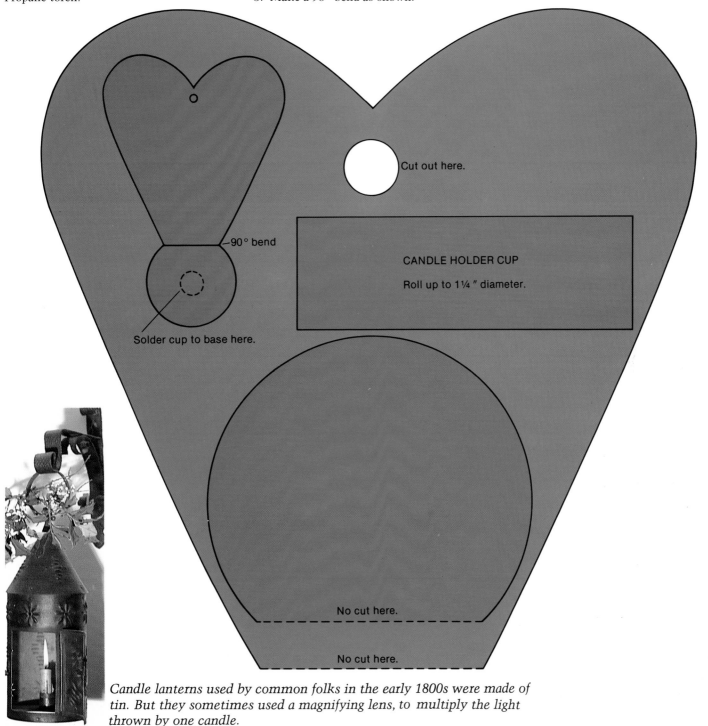

Cut out here.

90° bend

CANDLE HOLDER CUP

Roll up to 1¼ " diameter.

Solder cup to base here.

No cut here.

No cut here.

Candle lanterns used by common folks in the early 1800s were made of tin. But they sometimes used a magnifying lens, to multiply the light thrown by one candle.

Doves, almost always shown in pairs, are a symbol of love and peace used in folk art worldwide. This hollow tin sculpture is about one-and-a-half inches in thickness and two-feet wide. It was made around 1890 in Pennsylvania by a master tinsmith to demonstrate his skills and ornament his shop. Note the punchwork design.

The distelfink motif has enriched Pennsylvania Dutch needlework and other craft and artworks for generations. The word itself means goldfinch, but to the artisan it suggests a design in the form of a stylized bird or a pair of birds, such as this crewelwork embroidery.

Distelfink Crewelwork

A gift of lovingly embroidered needlework beautifully expresses affection and friendship. This happy portrait of two doves, in Pennsylvania Dutch distelfink style, symbolizes peace; the flowers represent beauty, the bright colors joy, and your contribution is love. The needlework technique used is crewel, a type of embroidery done in a free manner with a variety of stitches and yarn or thread in a subtle rainbow of colors.

Materials

½ yd. of unbleached linen or natural-color, firmly-woven cotton fabric.
Crewel wool, 1 card each of the following colors: light pink, medium rose, dark rose, dark turquoise, medium turquoise, medium aqua, medium French blue, dark French blue, medium olive green, dark olive green, medium rust, dark orange, dark yellow, brown.
Materials for framing (see Skills Pages).

Tools

Embroidery frame.
Crewel needle.
Scissors.
Tracing paper.

Dimensions

The finished picture is 6½ × 16 inches. Before you begin, see Skills Pages for detailed instructions on how to execute the following stitches: coral stitch, Holbein stitch, large straight stitch, laid stitch, cross-stitch, and star-filling stitch. Practice any stitches with which you are not familiar, using extra yarn and scrap fabric similar to that of the picture background.

Preparing the fabric

1. Trace the design on tracing paper, enlarging the diagram so that each small square equals ½ in. (See Skills Pages for instructions on enlarging patterns).
2. Cut a 12½ by 21½-in. rectangle out of the ½-yd. fabric.
3. Center the design on the fabric and transfer it.

Embroidering the design

1. Put the work in the embroidery frame. Begin to work the picture, following the photograph as a color guide. Use only one strand of wool yarn throughout.
2. The broken lines on the diagram indicate the coral stitch and the unbroken lines represent the Holbein stitch. The lines across each feather on the birds' tails are worked in a large straight stitch. All shaded areas are to be done in the laid stitch. After completing the star-shaped motifs using the star-filling stitch, use a small cross-stitch to hold the larger stitches of each star together.

Completing the picture

After finishing the embroidery, block and frame your work. See Skills Pages for detailed instructions.

A crowd of Amish dolls sits on a "mammy's bench," an unusual piece of furniture made especially for rocking youngsters. The mammy sat in the open space on the left and placed the infant safely behind the bars, which could be removed if a grownup wished to use it as a bench. This rare, left-handed example—made in England in 1830—is of pine, decorated with stenciled designs. The exploded view shows how it is constructed.

Swinging Cradle

Here's a project to start early in the fall; perhaps it could be gramp's gift for baby's first Christmas. If you lavish a little care in building and finishing, it will serve great- and great-great grandchildren as well.

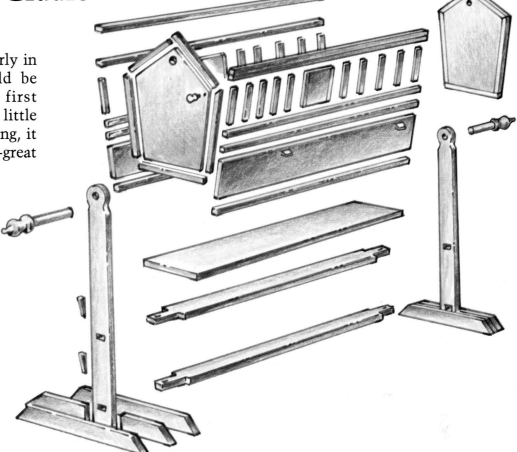

Parts Chart

Qty	Type of wood	Size	Description
2	2 × 6	53″	Side supports
2	2 × 6	48″	Center supports
4	2 × 6	26″	Outer base
4	2 × 6	10¼″	Inner base
2	¾″ plywood	19½″ × 27″	End panels
1	¾″ plywood	16″ × 37½″	Bottom
2	¾″ plywood	6″ × 11¼″	Center panels
2	¾″ plywood	5″ × 37½″	Side panels
2	1″ dowels	3½″	Cradle supports
2	¼″ dowels	1½″	Side stops
2	¼″ dowels	2½″	Cradle support stops
4	wood scraps	4″	Wedges
2	1″ finials		Cradle support ends
2	¼″ finials		Side stop ends
24	¾″ × ¾″	11¼″	Rails
10	¾″ × ¾″	37½″	Side frame

Note: the following parts do not appear with the pattern pieces.

2	¾″ × ¾″	13½″	End panel top trim
2	¾″ × ¾″	14½″	End panel top trim
4	¾″ × ¾″	18″	End panel side trim
2	¾″ × ¾	17½″	End panel bottom trim
2	¾″ × ¾″	20″	Bottom supports
2	¾″ × ¾″	10″	Bottom supports

Materials

Lumber: see parts chart.
Sandpaper, medium and fine grain.
Drill, with ½″, ⅜″, and ¼″ bits.
Two 1½″ or 2″ hinges with screws.
Wood glue.
Sabre saw, hammer.
1″ and 2″ nails.

Cutting and drilling

1. Cut out all of the pieces according to the dimensions of the patterns and in the quantity and type of wood shown on the parts chart.
2. Sand all pieces with medium- and then fine-grain sandpaper.
3. Drill holes where indicated; mortise the center and side supports.

Assembling the cradle

Use the exploded drawing at the top of this page as the basic guide for assembly.

1. Nail the inner bases, outer bases, and center supports together.

2. Nail and glue the trim pieces to each end panel. Attach a support for the cradle bottom to the inside of each panel; its position is shown on the end-panel pattern.

3. Assemble the top section of the side first. Nail rails to sides of center panel. Space other rails 2¼" apart on both sides of the center panel, and nail and glue two upper frame pieces and one lower frame piece in place.

4. Assemble the bottom section of the side. First, nail and glue the support to inside of side panel; position is shown on pattern. Next, nail and glue frame pieces to top and bottom of side panel.

5. Hinge bottom section to top section, so that the top opens out.

6. Assemble the other side in the same manner, but do not hinge the sections; nail and glue them together.

7. Nail and glue the side assemblies to the end panels. Nail through the end panel trim all the way up the rear side assembly. Nail only the bottom section of the front side to the end-panel trim, leaving the upper, hinged part free to open.

8. Drill ⅜" holes through the end-panel trim and side rail on the front side at both ends; see drawing, "Installing side stops". Insert ¼" dowel and finial in hole to hold hinged section in place.

9. Place bottom piece inside cradle, resting on supports.

10. Insert 1" dowels with large finials through holes at top of side supports and end panels to hang cradle. (See drawing, "Installing cradle supports and stops".) Drill ⅜" holes through tops of supports and ¼" into the dowels. Insert ¼" dowels to hold the 1" dowels in place.

Installing side stops

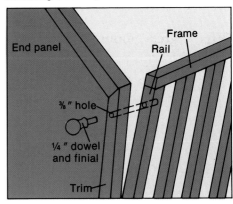

Installing cradle supports and stops

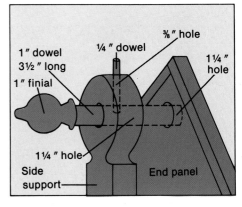

Finishing steps

Oil, varnish, or paint the cradle as you wish. Be sure that any paint you use is non-toxic.

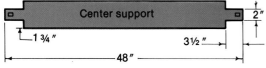

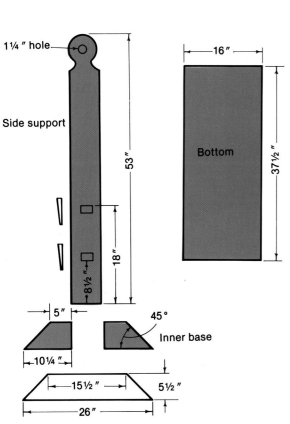

Side support

Bottom

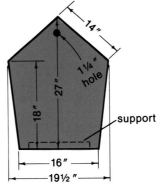

support

Outer base

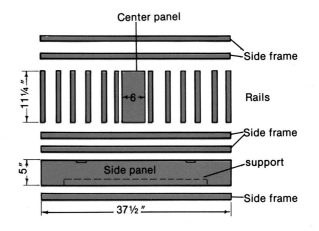

Hand-dipped Candles

What's great about candle making is that you use your imagination and creativity to choose colors, shapes, and scents. Here is a recipe for making both single and multicolored candles, and when you're through, you can turn them into holiday gifts by decorating them with holly leaves and berries.

Materials

The following can be purchased at an arts and crafts store or hobby shop:

Wicks—use, flat, loosely-braided ones for candles that drip, or square, tightly-braided ones for dripless candles.

Stearic acid crystals. This is a wax additive that makes stronger, longer-burning candles.

Dyes, in slab or powdered form. Wax crayons, which produce nice colors, can also be used. However, they leave a sediment that must be allowed to settle at the bottom of the wax before beginning the dipping or pouring process.

Scent oils.

Supplies

Paraffin (available at supermarkets).

Tall juice can, with smooth sides (without ridges). Use 2 or more cans for candles with multicolored layers.

Nuts, bolts, or other weights.

Saucepan.

Pencil, dowel rod, or wire coat hanger.

Sharp penknife.

Cutting and melting the paraffin

1. Cut the paraffin into pieces small enough to fit into the tall juice can.
2. Place the juice can in a saucepan that is half-filled with water. Put the paraffin pieces in the can and melt on the stove over low heat. Continue adding paraffin pieces until the melted mixture fills the can up to 2 inches from the top. Add scent oils sparingly since too much will cause improper mixing with the wax.
3. Add stearic acid crystals and dye (or crayons) to the wax and stir thoroughly. Be careful not to splash the wax around.

Dipping the candles

1. Suspend weights from the lengths of wick, hanging one or more from a pencil, dowel rod, or coat hanger.
2. Dip the wick into the wax repeatedly, but wait between each dip for the previous layer to solidify. Do not hold the candle in the can, but dip in and out in one fluid motion.
3. For a tapered candle, make each successive dip shallower than the preceding one.
4. When the diameter of the candle's base reaches one inch, trim off the bottom portion (with the weight attached) using a sharp knife. Dip the candle a final time.
5. Hang the candles up to harden for several hours.

To make a candle out of leftover paraffin

1. After the leftover wax in the can has hardened, remove it by running hot water over the outside of the can until the wax slides out.
2. Heat a straight length of the coat hanger and use it to poke a hole through the center of the wax.
3. Insert a wick into the hole and pour a little bit of melted wax around it.

To make candles with multicolored layers

Use two or more juice cans in the dipping process, with different colored dyes in each. Alternate colors after every five dips of the candle.

A country kitchen is full of intriguing smells and colors that inspire a candlemaker. Bayberry has scented candles since the Pilgrims landed; cinnamon, too, adds a pungent touch. The swag of bright apples and the strings of red peppers may appear on the tree when Christmas comes, but they will return to the kitchen for use in winter recipes. The finished candles have been hung to harden in pairs by their common wick.

The Maine craftsman who constructed this wooden weathervane around 1820 dramatically stylized the tail feathers. The natural feather-like texture was not his doing, though—the weather did that. The type of hinges used indicate that the vane was repaired much later in the nineteenth century.

This mid-nineteenth-century weathercock, although made to a standard pattern, was available in many sizes. This one is about 30 inches high. The body was cast to show moderate detail; the tail was cut out of sheet metal and attached after the detail had been hammered in; the feet were originally attached to a cross-perch.

Almost all old weathervanes have been battered and dented by branches, storms, and small boys' rocks. It is unusual to find a nineteenth- century vane free of bullet holes. This is the famous Blackhawk design horse, made around 1875. Its body is copper, which turns green when the weather oxidizes it. The head is zinc, a heavier metal, to balance the weight of the vane.

Rooster Weathervane

This pine and copper weathercock is patterned after a nineteenth-century, cast-iron barntopper, now in the Abbie Aldrich Rockefeller Folk Art Collection at Williamsburg. Made without the services of foundry, forge, or smithey, this modern counterpart will grow more picturesque as the body weathers to silvergray and the comb, wattle, tail, and feet oxidize to a green patina.

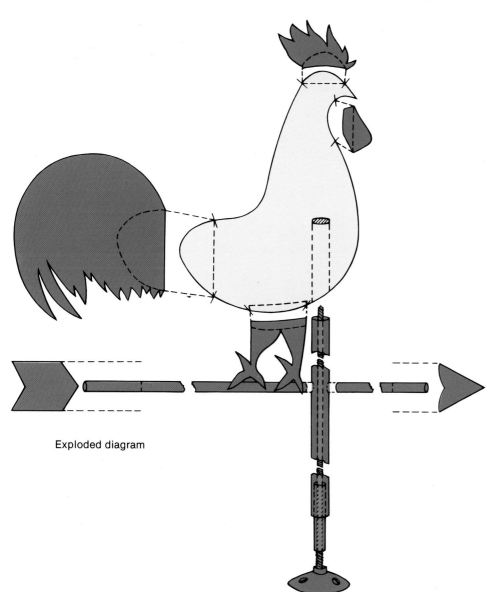

Exploded diagram

Materials
One 2 × 8 pine board, 10″ long.
One 8″ × 12″ copper sheet, 1/32″ thick.
3/8″ (outside diameter) soft copper tubing, 24″ long.
1/2″ (outside diameter) soft copper tubing, 18″ long.
1/4″ threaded rod, 3′ long.
Threaded flange for 1/4″ threaded rod.

Tools
Sabre or coping saw
Small screwdriver.
Tin snips.
Hammer.
Wood rasp.
Metal file.
Hacksaw.
Propane torch.
Solder and flax.
Sandpaper.
Stain for wood.
Clear-finish sealer for wood.
Electric drill with 1/2″ wood bore.
Epoxy glue.
Tracing paper.

Constructing the body

1. Trace the outline of body piece onto tracing paper and transfer to the 10-in. piece of 2 × 8 board. Cut out, using sabre or coping saw.
2. Round all edges with a rasp. DO NOT use the rasp on the beak. Next, smooth all rounded edges with sandpaper.
3. Transfer all letter markings from the pattern onto the body.
4. Saw slits, for the comb and tail, in the center of the body thickness. Stop sawing at the markings designated as ''A'' and ''A¹'' for the tail and ''B'' and ''B¹'' for the comb.
5. Chisel the slits, for the wattle and the legs, in the center of the body thickness from C to C¹ and from D to D¹. A small screwdriver works well for this.
6. In the center of the body thickness, drill a hole, ½ in. in diameter and 3½ in. deep; drill it at the ''X'' mark, at the angle shown on the body pattern. Make sure your measurements are correct.

Constructing the wattle, tail and legs

1. Trace the outlines of the wattle, tail and legs onto the tracing paper and transfer them to the copper sheet.
2. Cut out all the shapes with tin snips, then file the rough edges.
3. Put the shapes between boards (so you don't mar them) and flatten them with a hammer. Insert shapes in the slits on the body to make sure they fit.

Constructing the turnpost and arrow

1. Straighten the ⅜-in. and ¼-in. lengths of copper tubing.
2. Saw 1 in. off one end of the ½-in. tubing; next, de-burr the inside of the tubing.
3. Cut a circle ½-in. in diameter out of scrap copper and push it into the ½-in. hole in the body.
4. Smear small amount of epoxy glue onto untrimmed end of the ½-in. tubing that will be inside the body. Next, insert tubing all the way into the hole in body. If necessary, use the drill and borer to slightly widen the hole.
5. Cut an 8½-in. and 9½-in. length from the ⅜-in. copper tubing. Using hacksaw, cut a 1¼-in.-long slit in the 9-½-in. tube. (For precise sawing, first put a ¼-in. wood dowel inside the tubing to stiffen it.)
6. Trace the outlines of the arrowhead and feather onto tracing paper and transfer to copper sheet. The arrowhead is 2¼'' long by 2'' wide; the feather is 3'' long by 2¾'' in. wide.
7. Contour the unslit ends of the ⅜-in. tubing so they fit flush on the ½-in. tubing. Align the slits vertically.
8. Solder the arrowhead and feather into the slits on the arrow tubing.
9. Using epoxy, glue the feet into the slit on the wooden body.
10. Solder the feather end of the arrow to the turnpost and feet.
11. Put four 7-in. lengths of solder in the arrowhead tubing to provide balance.
12. Solder the head end of the arrow to the turnpost.
13. Cut a 17½-in. piece from the ¼-in. threaded rod. File or grind a point onto the cut end.
14. Screw the flat end of the threaded rod into the flange, then fasten the flange to the base.
15. Slide the remaining 6-in. length of the ⅜-in. tubing over the threaded rod.
16. Slide the turnpost over the rod and the ⅜-in. tubing.

Finishing

1. Stain the wood in the shade of your choice.
2. If desired, feather lines can be added to the tail by gently tapping a countersink punch with a hammer.
3. Glue the tail, comb, and wattle into the body slits.

Soldering hints

1. Clean the soldering iron until the tip is bright.
2. Plug in the iron; when it is hot, melt some solder onto the tip; this is called ''tinning.'' (1)
3. Clean the copper surfaces to be soldered, and be careful not to touch them (the oil from your fingers prevents the solder from sticking).
4. Heat the surfaces to be joined with the iron until they are hot enough to melt rosin-core solder when you apply it; it will flow over the areas that were cleaned. (2)

Note: if the solder does not stick, the surfaces were not properly cleaned, or your solder does not contain the correct rosin flux.

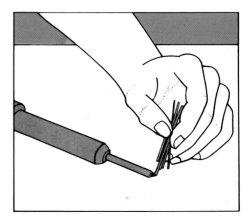

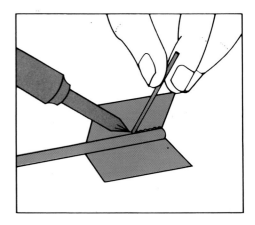

Press the iron against the copper until it is hot enough to melt the solder. Move the solder slowly along the joint just behind the iron.

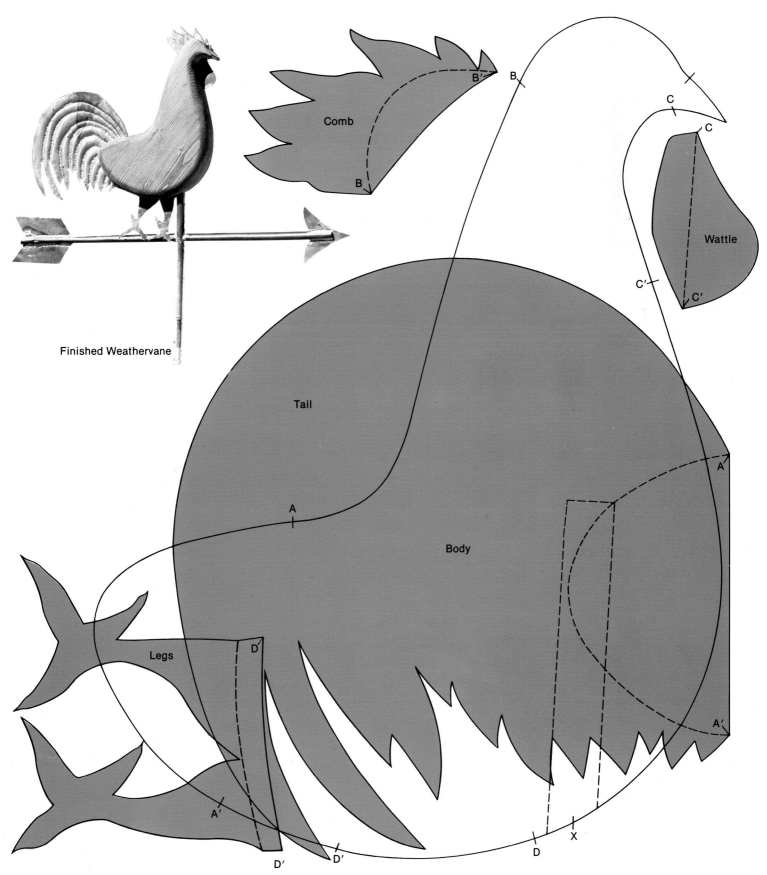

Finished Weathervane

Comb

Wattle

Tail

Body

Legs

❋ Sailor's Ropework Mat

This nautical doormat is made out of sisal rope that can be dyed the color of your choice. It requires only one knot: the Turk's head, or carrick bend, as sailors call it, and it's easy to make once you've mastered the step-by-step instructions given below.

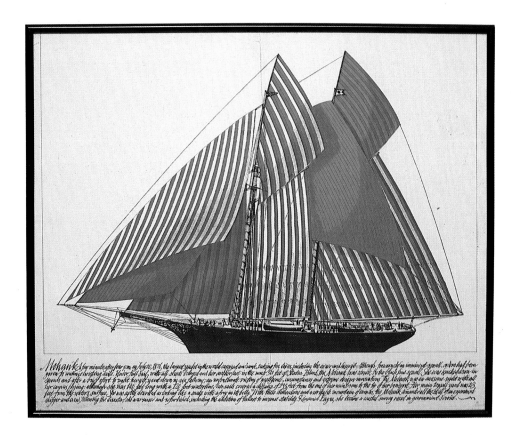

The legend for the picture above reads: "Mohawk. A few minutes after four p.m. on July 20, 1876, the largest yacht in the world capsized and sank, taking five lives, including the owner and his wife. Although forewarned of an imminent squall, orders had been given to continue hoisting sails. Under full sail, with all sheets belayed and her anchor fast in the mud 500 feet off Staten Island, the Mohawk was struck by the black line squall. She was knocked down in seconds and after a brief effort to right herself, went down in six fathoms; an unfortunate victim of negligence, circumstances and extreme design innovations. The Mohawk was an awesome sight with all her canvas flying; although she was 140 feet long with a 120 foot waterline, her sails covered a distance of 235 feet from the end of her main boom to the tip of her bowsprit. Her main topsail yard was 163 feet from the water's surface. She was aptly described as looking "like a snake with a frog in its belly." With these dimensions and a veritable mountain of canvas, the Mohawk demanded all the skill of an experienced skipper and crew. Following the disaster, she was raised and refurbished, including the addition of ballast to increase stability. Renamed Eagre, she became a coastal survey vessel in government service."

Materials and tools

110' of ½" sisal rope, for a 2' mat. (Use 225' of 1" rope for a 4' mat.) Sisal rope is a natural fiber that dyes well. If you don't care to dye your mat, you can substitute any number of other ropes, such as Manila hemp or cotton clothesline. However, keep in mind that synthetic fibers do not take dye well.
Small reel of monofilament plastic (fishing line).
Wide masking tape, black or any other color. Large, sturdy sewing needle, at least 3" long. A "stole weaving" needle is good to use.
Sharp knife.
Large piece of poster board or a table top for a working surface.

Materials needed if you choose to dye the mat

2 pkgs. of cold-water dye in color of your choice. Regular fabric dye can be used but the hot water is not as easy to work with.
Large container to mix the dyebath in. An old metal washtub is perfect.
Sturdy stick.
Pair of tongs.
Hammer (the bigger the better).

Tying the Turk's head knot

1. Pull off about 20 ft. of rope from the coil. This will be the working end that is used to make the outside of the mat.
2. Place the rope on the floor or whatever working surface you've chosen. Hold the end of the rope at the 20-ft. spot in one hand, and run the other hand about 4 ft.

down towards the loose end. Make an oval loop about 1½ ft. in diameter, with the loose end over the longer end.

3. Using the 20-ft. end, make a second loop on top of the first one, and bring the rope under the dark end of the first loop. Work above and to the left of the first loop.

4. Still using the same end, make a third loop opposite the first one. Thread the end over the top of the second loop, under the left side of the first loop, over the bottom of the second loop, and under the right side of the first loop.

5. To complete the knot, bring the same end around into a fourth loop, finishing next to the long end.

Making the mat

1. Using the long end and working on the inside, thread the rope through, following the other loops and increasing the layers. BE SURE to keep the entire knot completely flat while you work on it. Because the rope follows the inside of the loops, remember to keep the rope you are working with inside as you follow the knot around.

2. Continue winding the rope around until you have closed the spaces and have an even number of rows in each loop (the one shown has 8 rows).

3. Turn the mat over, cut the ends of the rope, and tuck them in so they are not visible on the top side.

Sewing the mat together

1. Use pieces of masking tape to keep the mat together while you sew it. This will help keep the loops in place and make the mat easier to handle.

2. Cut off about 6 ft. of the plastic line, knot one end, and thread the other end through the large needle.

3. Start at the outside of the mat on the wrong side and catch the top of all the ropes in each loop. Pull the thread through and work back toward the outside again. Repeat at three places in each of the four loops.

4. Sew the ends of the rope firmly in place so they won't ravel or pull loose.

5. At the four places where the loops cross each other, tack the mat together by sewing several stitches in the same place. Do this on both sides, so people won't catch their toes.

Dyeing the mat

1. Mix the dye according to the package's directions, using only enough water to submerge the mat. Remember, the less water you use, the more brilliant the color will be.

2. Use the stick to push the mat into the dyebath, making sure the entire mat is covered with dye so the color will penetrate evenly. Let the mat soak for 20 minutes and remember that it will look darker while wet.

3. Remove the mat, pour out the dyebath, refill the tub with water, and rinse the dyed mat for a few minutes to remove excess color. Place the mat on newspapers to dry.

4. Since rope tends to shrink when wet, the mat may not now lie as flat as it did. Use the hammer to pound any raised portions until they are level again.

5. Let the mat dry for 24 hours. Check it every now and then to see that it's drying in a proper form. If it pops up, hammer it down again.

Wind the cord around the inside of the loops until you have closed the spaces and have an even number of cords.

Tape the mat together for easier handling while sewing.

Catch the top of the cords with the needle, pull the plastic line through, then work back to the outside again.

Turk's head knot

1. Make the loop with the 20-ft. end (light) over the 90-ft. end (dark).

2. Make a second loop over the first one and bring the cord under the dark end of the first loop.

3. Make a third loop opposite the first one, then weave the cord through the other loops.

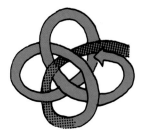

4. Complete the knot with a fourth loop that ends at the same place you started.

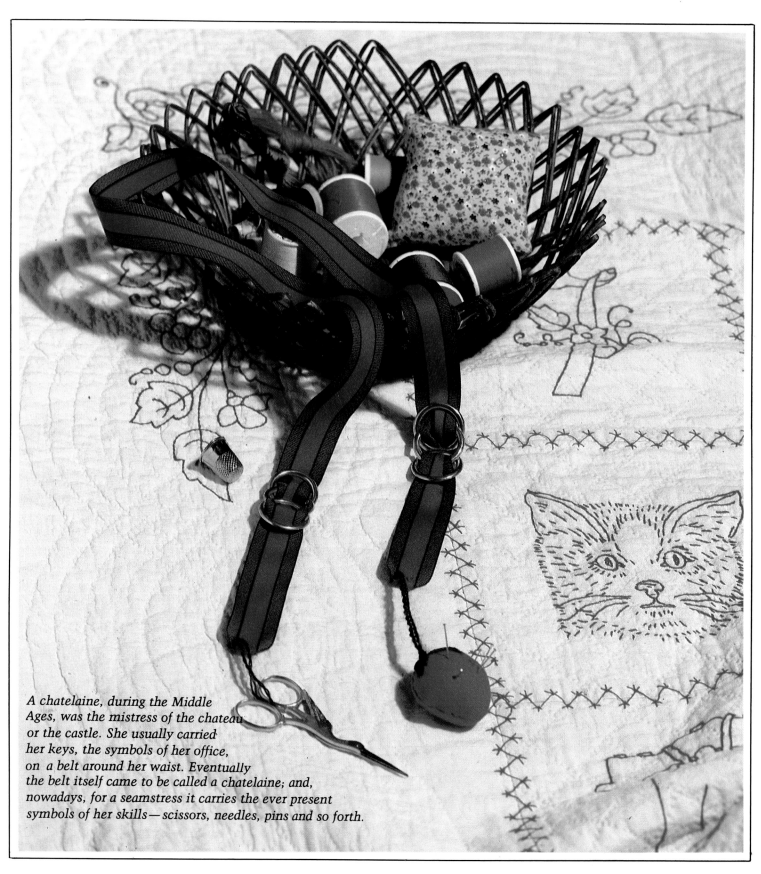

A chatelaine, during the Middle
Ages, was the mistress of the chateau
or the castle. She usually carried
her keys, the symbols of her office,
on a belt around her waist. Eventually
the belt itself came to be called a chatelaine; and,
nowadays, for a seamstress it carries the ever present
symbols of her skills—scissors, needles, pins and so forth.

Stitch along dotted line with right sides together.

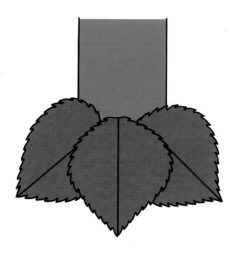

Stitch leaves together and to the ribbon along their top edges.

Attach 3 brass rings, 4" from each end.

 # Needleworker's Chatelaine

The Needleworker's Chatelaine hangs handily around your neck, keeping such tools as thread, needles, and embroidery scissors where you can put your hands on them without taking your eyes off your work. It's pretty, inexpensive, easy to make, and is a practical, welcome gift. Here's how to do it.

Two gossips sewing are caricatured in this old paper montage.

Materials

1 yd. ribbon, 3" wide.
6 metal curtain rings, ³⁄₁₆".
Red fabric scrap, 6" × 6".
Green felt scrap, 6" × 6".
Green yarn, 10"–15" length.
1 small metal snap-hook (optional).

Tools

Small sewing scissors.
Firm tracing paper.
Sewing machine (optional).
Needle.
Thread.
White glue.
Clean sand.

Assembling the strawberry

1. Transfer the strawberry shape to firm tracing paper, cut out the pattern, and then cut two berries out of the red cloth.
2. Firmly stitch the berry shapes together along seamline by hand or machine with right sides together.
3. Turn strawberry right-side-out, pack tightly with clean sand, and hand stitch the top closed.
4. Transfer the green berry top shape to paper and cut out of the green felt. Glue it onto the top of the berry.
5. Make a paper pattern of the leaf shape and cut out the six leaves from the green felt.
6. Stitch the leaves together into two groups of three leaves each.

Finishing the ribbon

1. Fold each ribbon end back ¼ in. and stitch across it.
2. Attach three of the metal rings four inches from each end.
3. Stitch one end of a 4-in. length of green yarn to the strawberry's stem and the other to one end of the ribbon.
4. Attach the embroidery scissors to the other end of the ribbon with green yarn. OR stitch the eye of a small snap-hook to the end of the ribbon.
5. Sew a group of felt leaves to each end of the ribbon.

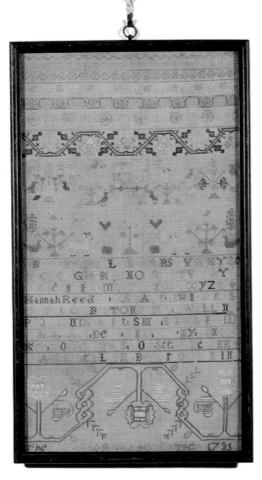

"Hannah Reed is my name New England is my Nation BOSTON is my dwelling place and Christ is my salvation..."

The work of Hannah Reed, dated 1735, is a classic example of why samplers were initially called "examplers." They served as important references for showing how various embroidery stitches were worked. After finishing her exampler, a young woman would roll it up to store in a drawer—like a reference book in a bookcase—until she needed to know how a particular stitch looked. Often, Englishmen would be called upon to teach the young women, and in doing so, defined sampler-making as a very prim, precise skill with no room for self-expression. Because the counting of stitches for each line was required, it was also a rigorous mathematical exercise. Hannah Reed's contains bands of two upper-case alphabets and one lower-case, along with birds, hearts, crowns, and sheep. Measuring 10½ inches wide by 18½ inches high, her sampler illustrates a superb command of each stitch.

"Go on I pray and Let Me Still Pursue Those Golden arts The Vulgar Never Knew"

After 1750, as the printing press became increasingly accessible and books affordable, it became more common for young women to learn how to read. Therefore, the exampler evolved into the more pictorial sampler. Isabella Hempstead's shows needlework that is remarkable not only in its quality but in the quantity and variety of stitches executed. Measuring 12 inches wide by 5½ inches high, it is dated 1776 and is probably of English origin.

Many times the quality of needlework itself was superior to the composition. Electa Bush's work shows a naive perspective (the rose and tree are as large as the house) that was common in early nineteenth-century samplers. Her sampler was made in 1818. Its federal house is a typical Bostonian style.

Elizabeth Margaret Crosthwaite's identity is unknown, but her antebellum cross-stitch sampler proves that she was an accomplished needlepoint artist at age twelve.

Cross-Stitch Sampler

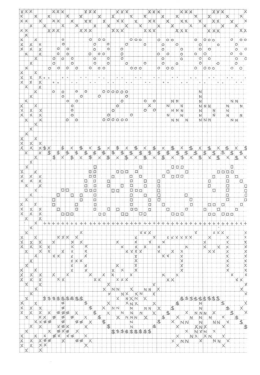

X	Dark Red
O	Light Beige
.	Light Sea Green
N	Khaki Green
$	Olive Green
□	Light Pink
+	Dark Beige
φ	Khaki Green
//	Peach
3	Light Peach
Z	Light Tan
■	Dark Royal Blue
·/.	Medium Blue
⊠	Dark Grey
.·	Off White

A sampler was used as a teaching tool to instruct little girls in their letters and numbers. After they had learned to stitch the alphabet and the border, they could try their own designs. In the early days, when pattern books did not exist, traditional themes were handed down from mother to daughter. Houses, flowers, birds, and pets were popular. We don't know who Elizabeth Margaret Crosthwaite was, but her sampler was done on a canvas known as Penelope, using wool yarn rather than floss. To simulate the antique look, you might choose a linen with 27 threads per inch (about 14 stitches per inch) or 14-count aida cloth, which is available in needlework stores.

Materials and supplies

Piece of needlework canvas or linen, approximately 25″ × 25″.
Needlework thread in the colors listed in the Color Key.
Sewing thread.
Embroidery frame.
Fine tapestry needle.
Picture frame.

Directions

1. Overcast the edges of the linen or cotton fabric to keep it from fraying; then mount it in the embroidery frame. (Canvas does not need to be overcast or mounted.)
2. Flower thread is matte finished and is thus most like the original sampler; use one strand in the needle. Use two strands of DMC thread.
3. Each square on the chart indicates a cross-stitch (see the Skills Pages for needlepoint stitches).
4. Use the first alphabet in the sampler to write your own name, age, and date.
5. See Skills Pages for instructions for blocking and framing. (For more information and to locate the shop nearest you that sells the supplies you need, write to Ginnie Thompson Originals, P.O. Box 99, Pawleys Island, SC 29585.)

Danish Flower Thread	DMC Article 117
500	321
7	642
302	3013
212	731
34	733
113	758
213	632
212	730
95	922
93	945
250	422
202	823
226	924
215	3022
16	739

❄ Potpourries

To capture the perfume of the summer season for year-long pleasure, try making potpourries and sachets to scent closets and drawers and to ornament your bureau; or share the enjoyment by giving them as gifts with that special home-made touch to family and friends. "Potpourrie," a French word, means a mixture, such as a medley of songs, a meat stew, or in this case, a pot of dried and preserved flower petals, leaves, seeds, berries, and roots, tempered and preserved with oils and spices. The mixture is placed in a perforated container, or better, a transparent, open-topped jar, to let you see the rich but subtle colors as well as smell the lovely fragrance, which acts as a natural room freshener. A "sachet" is a potpourri mixture in a little muslin bag, which is placed in a drawer or closet to scent clothing and linen.

There are myriad potpourri recipes, some of which contain exotic ingredients. Here is a simple recipe which you may vary as you wish.

There are two secrets to making successful sachets: Make the fragrance so attractive that you would want your own lingerie drawer to smell that way; then make "the little bag" (which is what "sachet" means in French) so pretty that anyone you give it to will love you all over again each time she opens her drawer and sees it there.

Materials

1 qt. flower petals. If you pick them from flowers that are about to bloom, their fragrance will last longer. Choose them for color as well as fragrance. Try roses, carnations, geraniums, honeysuckle, lavender, lilacs, and perhaps a few leaves of herbs, such as mint or rosemary.
1 oz. of spices, such as clove, nutmeg, mace, cinnamon, allspice, and brown sugar.
1 oz. of fixative, such as powdered orrisroot, tonka bean, calamus, cus-cus, dried ground citrus peel, angelica root, or gum benzoin.
Oil. Oil of rose, oil of lavender, or other aromatic oils are available from druggists.
Salt (optional, for drying).

Drying the petals

There are two drying methods:
1. Spread the petals out in a dark, airy room. If you turn them over every day or so, they will dry completely in about a week.

2. Put about an inch of salt in a cake tin and place the petals on top; sprinkle lightly with salt until completely covered. Put the tin out in the sun for several days, or put it in the oven under low heat for an hour or two. (The heat speeds up the absorption of the moisture in the petals by the salt.) When the petals are dry, remove the salt and store them in airtight containers.

Preparing other ingredients

1. Grind the spices and fixative to a coarse powder in a mill or with a mortar and pestle. Add a few drops of oil and mix together; smell the mixture, and add oil sparingly until the odor pleases you. Store the mixture in an airtight container for a week or two.
2. Add the spice and oil mixture to the dried flowers, stirring gently with a wooden rod. Place the finished potpourri in a perforated container or a glass jar. To make a sachet, place about ½ cup in a small bag and tie or sew the mouth closed.

When carefully dried, many flowers retain their brilliant colors indefinitely. Cornflower, delphinium, zinnia, peony, strawflower, chrysanthemum, bittersweet, sumac, marigold, and rose, among others, make beautiful bouquets or, if treated with spices and oils, become fragrant potpourries and sachets.

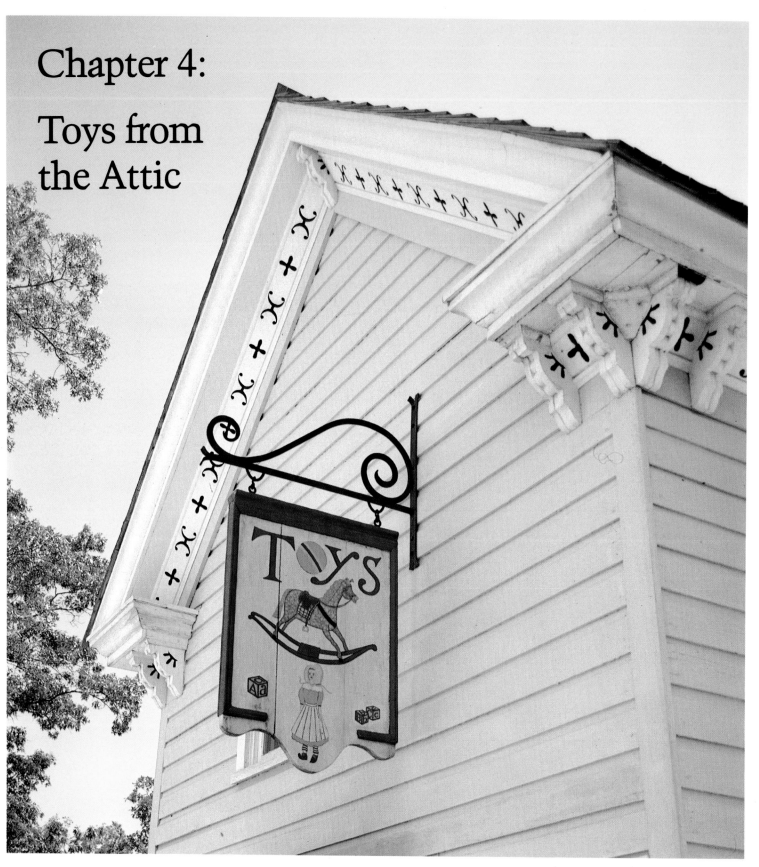

Chapter 4:

Toys from the Attic

Fire-Engine Toy

Here comes the old-fashioned fire truck. Kids love it, so look out—you may end up becoming the local fire-engine toy factory. The 17-inch pull toy can be made in one afternoon with inexpensive 1 x 12 pine, using either hand or small power tools.

When the toy fire engine has put out all the fires around the Christmas tree, take it and its young owner down to the fire house for an inspection tour of the real thing.

This fire engine would delight any child, but its owner decided to preserve it under glass, rather than let it be played with as a toy. It was built in the 1920s by a Mr. Crower from Waukesha, Wisconsin, who used household items to add details to the model. A careful inspection reveals the head of a ladies' hat pin on the fireman's helmet, upholstery tacks on the dashboard, bottle lids for the headlights, sewing-thread spools and bullet shells for fire extinguishing equipment, coat hangers and copper wiring for the railing, and chair slides for the tire hubcaps. The truck itself is made of wood, measures ten inches in length, and retains its original "fire-engine red" coat of paint.

Materials

White pine board: 4' of 1 x 12 board. The board actually measures ¾" x 11¼".
One 4¼" piece of 2 x 4 lumber (which actually measures 1½" x 3½").
Wood dowels: 6' of ⅜" dowel and 2' of 1¼" dowel.
4 washers with at least ⁷⁄₁₆" holes.
Glue–ordinary white or aliphatic resin.
Paint–½ pt. each of red and dark-gray acrylic, glossy latex enamel.

Tools

Drill, with a ⅜" bit and a ⁷⁄₁₆" bit that has at least a 2½" drilling depth.
Jackknife or rasp.
2 or 3 sheets each of medium- and fine-garnet sandpaper.
Small paintbrush (1½" or 2") and a fine-tipped artist's brush.
Hammer and nail set.
A "circle-cutter" attachment, (2¼") for a ¼" electric drill (optional).

Cutting the pieces

Draw the dimensions carefully and cut beside the lines so the thickness of the saw blade does not reduce the size of the final pieces. Square off the end of the board before you measure.

1. Measure and cut 18 pieces from the pine board. The figure shows one way to do this so the grain of the wood in each piece will run in the correct direction. This layout also allows you to cut out pieces with the same dimension in continuous, straight saw cuts. Then measure and cut out the individual pieces and the wheels.
2. Cut the circular windows out of the sides and back of the cab. Use a circle cutter if you have one. If not, start the cut by drilling a hole inside the circle, near the edge and big enough to insert the blade of a hand coping saw or electric sabre saw.
3. Cut the piece of 2 x 4 wood to a length of 4¼ inches for the hood (1½ in. by 3½ in. by 4¼ in.).

Drilling the holes

1. Drill ⁷⁄₁₆" holes for the axles straight through the narrow ¾-in. edge of the floor board from one side to the other. Drill the front axle hole 1½ inches in from the front end, and the rear axle hole 2¼ inches in from the rear end of the floor board.
   Drilling these holes absolutely straight is the only really tricky part of making this toy. This enclosed axle will stand up better

than the easier alternative of u-shaped staples nailed underneath the floor board.
   Drill halfway through from each side. The drill bit will have to be at least 2½ inches long because the rear end of the floor board is 5 inches wide.

TIP: Draw a sight line with a pencil across the width of the board from hole-center to hole-center. Tip the board up on its narrow, ¾-in. edge, and drill straight down sighting along the line. To help keep the drill hole true in the narrow dimension, drill through the exact center of a perfectly right-angled block to use as a starter guide. Hold it firmly on the edge of the board over the point to be drilled and drill through the block to get the axle hole started straight. Try this system on a scrap piece first to get the hang of it.

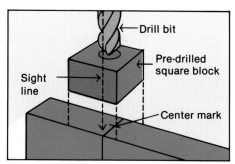

Use a square, pre-drilled block as a guide for drilling straight holes.

2. Drill six ⁷⁄₁₆-in. holes through the floor board for the firemen's pegs. Don't drill into the axle. This project specifies four firemen so a child can move them into different positions.
3. Drill two ⅜-in. holes about halfway through the thickness of the truck sides near the two top corners for the pegs to hold the ladders. Drill ⅞ inch down from the top of the side board, 1¾ inches in from the back end, and 1 inch in from the front.
4. Drill 8 evenly spaced, ⅜-in. holes through the 12-in. sides of the ladders for the rungs. To line these up evenly, tack or tape two 12-in. sides together and drill through both of them. Leave them together until you insert the rungs.
5. Drill a ⅜-in. hole through the center of each of the four wheels.
6. Drill a ⅜-in. hole about ½-in. into the front of the 2-in. by 4-in. hood piece for the hood ornament.

Assembling the truck

1. Sand the rough saw edges and splintery or sharp corners on the wood pieces.
2. Glue each piece before you nail it. Drive nails about ⅛ inch above the surface so you don't leave hammer marks. Recess them just under the surface with a nail set so the paint will fill in the holes.
3. Assemble the cab separately, then attach it as a unit to the floor board. Glue the hood ornament into its socket.
4. Cut and glue four 1¼-in. long dowel pegs into their sockets on the truck sides for the ladders. Sand them down if they are too snug to tap in lightly.
5. Nail the truck sides (peg holes outside) to the floor board, set 1 inch in from the outside edges of the floor to allow clearance between the ladder and wheels.
6. Cut the 5½-in. front axle and the 7-in. rear axle from ⅜-in. dowel. Run them through their holes in the floor board. Slip on the washers. Attach the wheels with a spot of glue and sand the ends flush with the wheels. Paint the wheels before attaching them. (3)

Assembling the ladders

1. Cut 16 of the 3¼-in. long rungs.
2. Dip one end into glue, and tap them through, flush. If the rungs don't go through easily with a light tap of a hammer, sand the end of the dowel narrower.
3. Glue the other ends of the dowels and fit the other side down over the rungs, flush.

Making the firemen

1. Cut four 5-in. pieces of 1¼-in. dowel.
2. Find the center of one end and drill a ⅜-in. hole straight down into that end to a depth of 1 inch.
3. Round the other end with a carving knife or rasp to make the head. Sand it smooth.
4. Cut four 1¾-in. lengths of ⅜-in. dowel. Dip one end in glue and tap it into the hole in the base of each fireman.

Painting

You will not need to sand between the two coats if you use latex enamels.

1. Paint all sides of the pieces, at least one coat, before you assemble them.
2. Paint the faces, hair, coats, collars and buttons of the firemen the way you think a child wants a fireman to look.

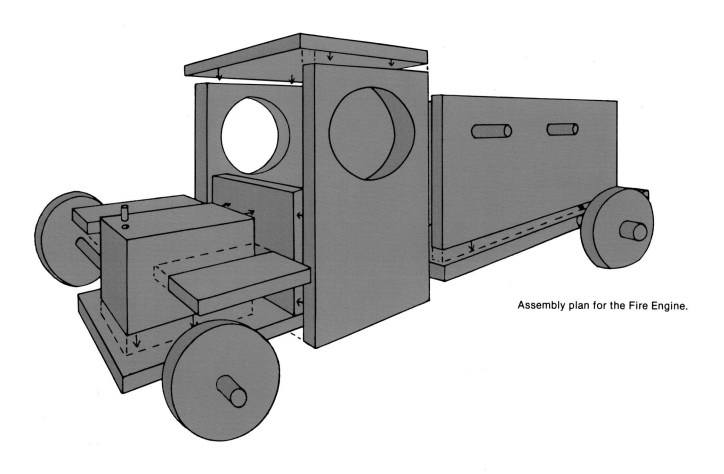

Assembly plan for the Fire Engine.

This plan shows how to cut the 18 pieces required for this project, out of a 1-in. by 12-in. board at least 40 inches long, so that the grain runs correctly.

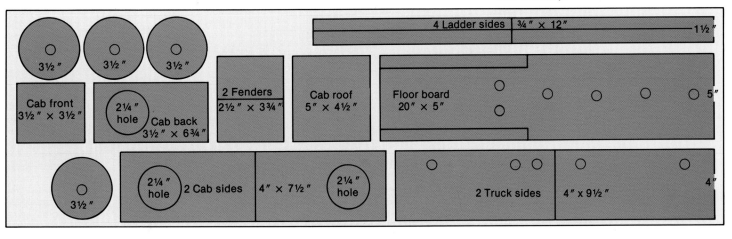

Whirligigs have been New England folk artists' way of making the wind tell its direction and entertain you at the same time. More than a century ago, this sailor, dressed like a Jolly Jack Tar, was a weathervane that stretched his arms into the Atlantic winds. He may have twirled a pair of paddles or, less likely because they were more fragile, oars.

☀ Nantucket Whirligig

Although many whirligigs are made with plain pieces of lath as blades, this Nantucket sailor wields a more appropriate pair of carefully-carved oars. The secret for making him whirl energetically in any breeze is to shape and mount the oars exactly as the plans indicate, since the angle at which the oar blades face the wind is crucial.

For strength in the shaft, each oar is whittled out of a solid piece of wood stock, with the blades turned slightly to catch the wind. As an easier and less fragile alternative, try solid, flat paddles.

Materials

2 or more 3″ lengths of ¾″ or 1″ dowel rod. (A broom or mop handle of pine works best.)
18″ length of 1 × 6 pine board (¾″ thick).
4″ × 12″ piece of ½″ thick pine board.
1 flattened tin can.
36″ length of ³/₁₆″ metal rod.
8″ length of ⅛″ metal rod (cut from a suit hanger).
Electric drill and bits.
Sabre saw with fine scroll-cutting blade and metal-cutting blade.
Tin snips or large utility shears.
Whittling knife.
Hammer.
Flat file.
Thin brads, ¾″ or 1″ long.
Yellow carpenter's wood-glue.
Epoxy glue.
Sandpaper.
Paint and small brushes.

Saw a bevel across the top half of the back of the head. The hat brim and ribbon are snipped from tin. The crown is a wood disk screwed or nailed through its center and through the center of the brim into the beveled surface to hold it permanently on the back of the sailor's head.

1. Trace body (joining pattern at waist), shoes, hat brim, hat crown circle, and oars from book onto paper.

2. Transfer body shape onto ¾ in.-thick pine; shoes, hat crown, and oars onto ½ in.-thick pine, and hat brim onto flattened sheet metal from the tin can.

3. Cut out wooden shapes with sabre saw, using the fine scroll blade; cut hat brim from sheet metal with tin snips or heavy utility shears. Sand wooden pieces to slightly round the edges and remove saw-blade marks; file the hat brim to dull the sharp edges.

4. Drill ⅛-in. or ⁵⁄₃₂-in. axle hole through shoulder area of body shape. This hole must be level and centered.

5. Drill ⁷⁄₃₂-in. or ¼-in. pivot hole into body, again taking care to drill straight and true. After drilling, drive a nail with a flat head into the hole to act as the spinning surface for the pivot rod.

6. Measure 1⅜ in. down from the top of the sailor's head and draw a line straight across. Cut and sand away the shaded area shown on the pattern page to allow the hat brim and crown to be tacked on at the proper angle.

7. Whittle the two oars, making the blades as thin and lightweight as possible.

8. Cut two 3-in. lengths of ¾-in. or 1-in. dowel rod and drill a ³⁄₃₂-in. hole into one end of each. The holes must be centered so that the arms will spin properly on the whirligig. Test for a correctly centered hole by spinning each drilled dowel on the drill. If the hole is off-center and the spinning dowel wobbles, try again with another length of wood.

9. Once arm holes are drilled on-center, mount a slightly larger bit on your drill and push it into the arm hole as far as it will go. Turn on the drill briefly to make sure that the arm will not come off. BE SURE TO WEAR SAFETY GOGGLES. When the arm spins without wobbling, it is as though it were on a lathe, and you can hold a wood rasp, a craft knife, or coarse sandpaper lightly against the spinning arm to shape it to the dimensions given.

10. When the arms are complete, cut an oar notch on the end of each arm as shown in the pattern drawing.

11. Cut a piece of straight ⅛-in. metal rod 7 in. long and insert it through the axle hole in the body. Be sure the axle rod turns freely in the arm hole. Mix a small amount of epoxy and put some in each arm hole and on each end of the rod. Then insert the rod into each arm hole.

12. Before the epoxy sets, mark the center points of both oars by balancing them one at a time on a ruler edge. With the front of the sailor facing you, fasten an oar on the left side. The left oar blade should be up and fastened with a ¾-in. brad and a dab of glue at the angle shown on the pattern page. Temporarily fasten the second oar to the right side with tape, pointing the oar blade down. Move the second oar in its slot until the arms are balanced. Then turn it to the proper angle and fasten it with a brad and glue. The final step is to turn the arms on the axle until the oars are lined up together —one blade up, one blade down—when viewed from the side.

13. Fasten each shoe and the hat in place with a ¾-in. brad and a dab of glue.

14. File a point on one end of the ³⁄₁₆-in. metal pivot rod and check to see that the whirligig rotates on it freely.

15. Use enamel paint if you plan to put your sailor outdoors. His hat, shoes, and belt are black; his pants and kerchief are white; and his jersey is blue. The oars should be white with red tips. The hands and feet can be left natural and then varnished after the facial features have been painted on.

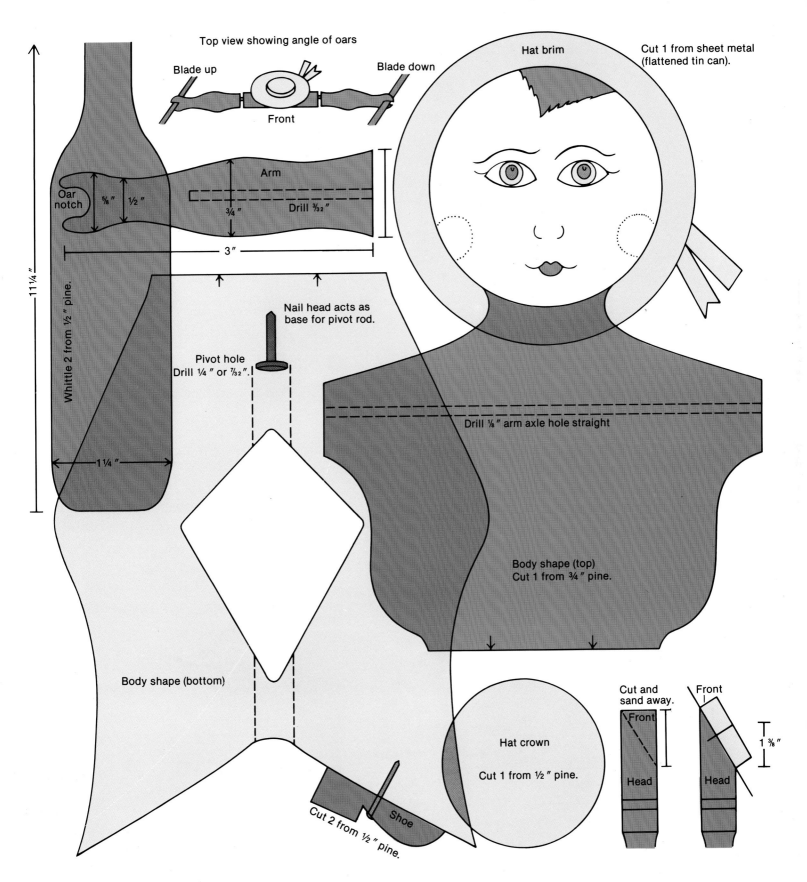

Top view showing angle of oars

Blade up

Blade down

Front

Oar notch

⅝″ ½″

Arm

¾″ Drill ³⁄₃₂″

3″

11¼″

Whittle 2 from ½″ pine.

1¼″

Hat brim

Cut 1 from sheet metal (flattened tin can).

Nail head acts as base for pivot rod.

Pivot hole
Drill ¼″ or ⁷⁄₃₂″.

Drill ⅛″ arm axle hole straight

Body shape (top)
Cut 1 from ¾″ pine.

Body shape (bottom)

Hat crown

Cut 1 from ½″ pine.

Cut and sand away.

Front

Front

Front

1 ⅜″

Head

Head

Shoe

Cut 2 from ½″ pine.

Here's a traditional toy train that really works: you can fill up the tender with candies to fuel the young engineer, then turn him loose to load up the freight cars and the automobile carrier before he chugs off to the next station. Cranking the authentic-looking crane is an especially satisfying operation.

Old-Fashioned Train

This homemade toy recalls the days when steam engines and passenger coaches regularly puffed and rattled through the towns and countryside of America and children ran to watch the mail train thunder past the grade crossing. The crane car and auto carrier are modern additions to this nineteenth-century train, but children who crank the levers and load the automobiles will not mind the anachronism. Whether you build only the five old-fashioned cars or all seven, any child will be delighted to pull them around the house. If your woodworking skills are a little rusty, read the Skills Pages for a thorough refresher course.

This interesting model railroad engine with working snow plow was probably made by, or for, an inventor as a patent model. The simplicity of the wooden locomotive characterizes good, American folk design. On the other hand, the plow's intricate mechanism explicitly demonstrates how it clears snow off the rails and throws it to each side of the track by means of the rotating vertical paddles.

Materials, tools, and supplies

Pine lumber: see chart.
Dowels: see chart.
30 washers with ⅝" hole.
Sabre saw.
Electric drill with ¼", ½", and 1" bits.
Wood rasp.
Hammer.
1" finishing nails.
Sandpaper, medium- and fine-grade.
Wood glue.

Cutting and drilling

Enlarge the pattern pieces from the grid (see Skills Pages for instructions).
Car beds:
1. Cut the 8-ft. 2 × 4 to 2⅝" wide.
2. Trace the engine, caboose, and the five other identical bed shapes onto the wood and cut out with the sabre saw.
3. Cut the rounded ends where indicated on the bed patterns.

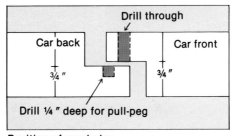

Position of peg holes

4. On the round end of the engine bed drill a hole ¼" deep for the pull peg. On the round end of the caboose bed drill the hole through. On all other beds drill a hole through on the front end and a hole ¼" deep on the rear end.

5. Drill a 1" hole through the crane car bed where indicated for the swivel dowel.
6. Drill 1" holes ½" deep in the passenger car bed and caboose bed for passengers.
Axles:
1. Cut five ½" axles, 5" long, for the crane car and engine.
2. Cut ten ½" axles, 6" long, for the other cars.
3. Cut eight ¼" axles, 2⅜" long, for the tiny cars.
Wheels:
1. From the 1 × 8 lumber, cut 28 wheels 2½" in diameter and 2 wheels 2" in diameter. Drill a ½" hole in the exact center of each wheel.
2. Cut sixteen ⅜" sections from 1" dowel for the tiny car wheels.

Materials Chart

	Size	Quantity	Used For
Lumber	2 × 4	8'	car beds
	2 × 6	2'	crane body, tiny cars, caboose upper level, cowcatcher
	1 × 8	4'	wheels
	¼" × 4"	6"	engine light and smokestack platform
	½" × 6"	14'	other pieces
Dowels	½"	9'	axles, pull pegs, crane turning pegs
	¼"	3'	tiny car axles
	1"	3'	smokestack, tiny car wheels, crane swivel dowel

Parts Chart

Car	Qty	Part	Lumber
Engine	1	Cab roof	½" lumber
	2	Cab sides	½" lumber
	1	Cab front	½" lumber
	1	Light	½" lumber
	1	Smokestack platform	¼" lumber
	1	Bed	2" lumber
	1	Cowcatcher	2" lumber
	4	Large wheels	¾" lumber
	2	Small wheels	¾" lumber
	1	Whistle	½" dowel, 1¼" long
	1	Smokestack	1" dowel, 1¼" long
	1	Lamp	½" dowel, ¼" thick
	1	Boiler	3" wood cylinder, 6½" long
	3	Axles	½" dowels, 4¾" long
	1	Pull peg	½" dowel, 1¼" long
	2	Side cylinders	1" dowel, 1¾" long
Tender	2	Sides	½" lumber
	1	Back	½" lumber
	1	Bed	2" lumber
	4	Large wheels	¾" lumber
	2	Axles	½" dowels, 6" long
	1	Pull peg	½" dowel, 1¼" long
Automobile Carrier	1	Upper level	½" lumber
	4	Side supports	½" lumber
	1	Bed	2" lumber
	4	Large wheels	¾" lumber
	2	Auto holders	¼" dowel, 2¾" long
	2	Axles	½" dowel, 6¼" long
	1	Pull peg	½" dowel, 1¼" long
	2	Auto bodies	¾" lumber
	1	Limousine body	¾" lumber
	1	Pickup body	¾" lumber
	8	Axles	¼" dowel, 2" long
	16	Tiny wheels	1⅜" dowel, ½" thick, with ¼" center hole
Caboose	1	Bed	2" lumber
	1	Upper level	2" lumber
	1	Roof	½" lumber
	2	Sides	½" lumber
	1	Upper level roof	½" lumber
	2	Front/Back	½" lumber
	4	Large wheels	¾" lumber
	2	Axles	½" dowels, 6" long
Passenger Car	1	Passenger	1" dowel, 2½" long
	2	Sides	½" lumber
	1	Bed	2" lumber
	1	Roof	½" lumber
	2	Front/Back	½" lumber
	4	Large wheels	¾" lumber
	2	Axles	½" dowels, 6" long
	1	Pull peg	½" dowel, 1¾" long
	2	Passengers	1" dowels, 2½" long
Crane Car	1	Inner body	½" lumber
	2	Outer body	2" lumber
	1	Lever	½" lumber
	1	Bed	2" lumber
	1	Swivel base	½" lumber
	4	Large wheels	¾" lumber
	1	Outer turning peg	½" dowel, 1½" long
	1	Inner turning peg	½" dowel, 4½" long
	1	Bottom swivel dowel	1" dowel, 4" long
	1	Holding pin	¼" dowel, 2" long
	2	Axles	½" dowel, 5" long
	1	Pull peg	½" dowel, 1¾" long
Freight car	1	Bed	2" lumber
	2	Sides	½" lumber
	2	Ends	½" lumber
	2	Axles	½" dowels, 6" long

Note: Large wheels are 2½" in diameter with ½" center holes. Small wheels are 2" in diameter with ½" center holes.

Engine boiler:
1. Cut 8 circles, 3" in diameter, from the 1 × 8 lumber.
2. Glue the circles together to form the boiler; let dry.
3. Saw off ¼" from one side of the boiler to make a flat surface for gluing the engine bed.

Smokestack platform: Cut out of ¼" lumber.

Caboose upper level, crane outer body pieces, tiny car bodies, and cowcatcher: Cut all pieces out of 2 × 6 lumber.

All other shapes:
Cut out of ½" lumber. Cut cowcatcher in half on the diagonal. Drill holes to start sabre-saw blade for cutting the caboose and passenger car windows.

Smokestack—Cut a 2" length from 1" dowel.
Pull Pegs—Cut six 1¼" lengths from ½" dowel.
Auto holders—Cut two 2" lengths from ¼" dowel.

Sanding the pieces

Sand all of the pieces until the edges are smooth, using medium- and then fine-grade sandpaper.

On pieces that need rounding, such as the wheels, use the wood rasp before sanding.

Assembling the pieces

Tender, passenger car, auto carrier, crane car, freight car, and caboose:
1. Use the drawings as guides. Glue and nail the side pieces to the sides of the car bed.
2. Add front, top, and back pieces where indicated.
3. Glue auto holders in place on the auto carrier upper level.
4. Glue upper compartment and compartment roof to the top of the caboose.

Engine:
1. Use the drawing as a guide. Glue the smokestack platform to the boiler and let it dry.
2. Glue boiler to the engine bed and let it dry.
3. Glue and nail cab front to the rear of the boiler. Attach sides and top of cab.
4. Glue the smokestack and the lamp to the platform. Glue the cylinders to the sides of the bed, leaving room for the small front wheel. Glue the whistle to the top of the cab. Glue cowcatcher to front of bed so that it points downward.

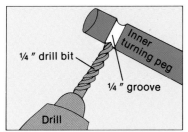

Crane:

1. Use the drawing as a guide. Glue the outer body pieces to the inside piece, one on either side.

2. Drill a hole for the crane lever, and then construct the lever as shown in the diagram.

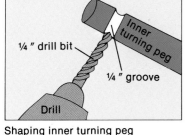

Shaping inner turning peg

Crane lever mechanism rear view

3. Tie a piece of string to the lever dowel between the outer pieces; run the end of the string through the hole at the top of the crane arm.

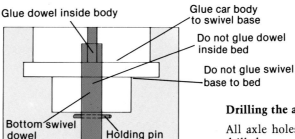

Crane swivel mechanism rear view

4. Glue and nail the swivel base to the crane body bottom. Drill a hole 1" deep and 1" in diameter; glue the swivel dowel in the hole.

5. Put the crane body on the bed with the swivel dowel projecting through the hole in the bed. Insert the holding pin through the dowel.

Drilling the axle holes

All axle holes on the large cars should be drilled approximately 5/8" in diameter so that the axles won't bind. Axle holes on the tiny cars should be about 3/8" in diameter. Make sure all holes are drilled straight.

1. Axle holes for the engine and the crane are drilled through the beds. Use the drawings as guides. The axle hole for the small wheels on the engine must be set slightly lower than those for the large wheels, so that all wheels touch the ground.

2. Axle holes for the other cars are drilled through the sides and the beds. Use the markings on the patterns for the sides to locate the centers of the holes.

Final steps

1. Insert the axles in the holes and place a washer over each end. Attach wheels to axles with a small amount of glue.

2. Glue pull-pegs in their holes.

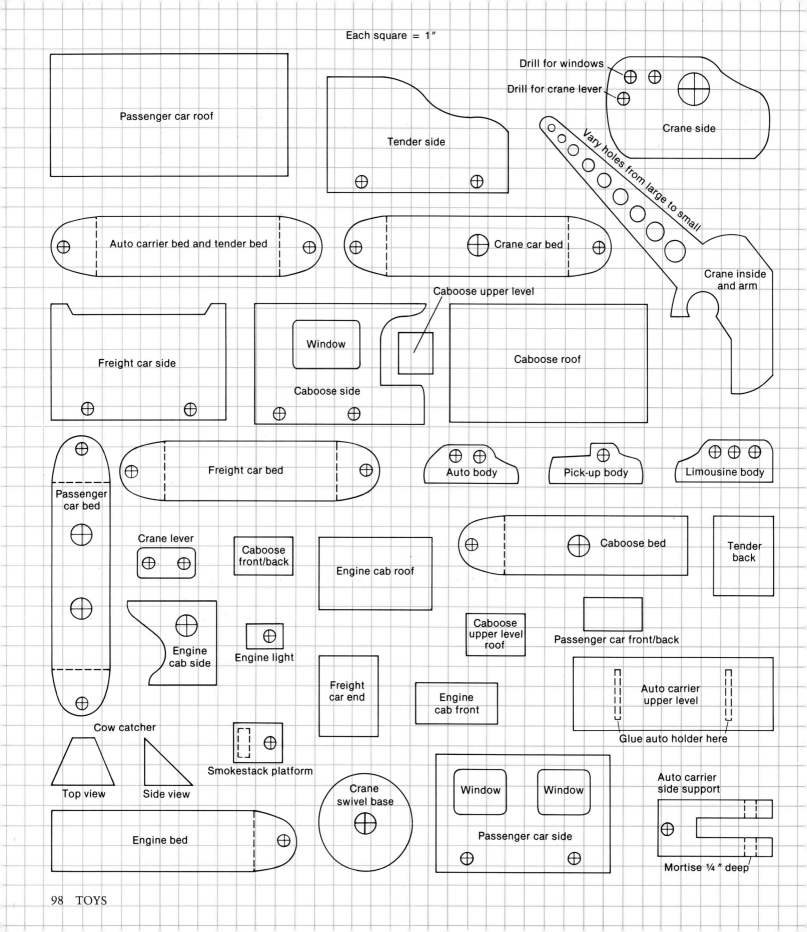

Each square = 1″

Passenger car roof

Tender side

Drill for windows

Drill for crane lever

Crane side

Vary holes from large to small

Auto carrier bed and tender bed

Crane car bed

Crane inside and arm

Freight car side

Window

Caboose side

Caboose upper level

Caboose roof

Passenger car bed

Freight car bed

Auto body

Pick-up body

Limousine body

Crane lever

Caboose front/back

Engine cab roof

Caboose bed

Tender back

Engine cab side

Engine light

Caboose upper level roof

Passenger car front/back

Cow catcher

Freight car end

Engine cab front

Auto carrier upper level

Glue auto holder here

Top view

Side view

Smokestack platform

Auto carrier side support

Engine bed

Crane swivel base

Window

Window

Passenger car side

Mortise ¼″ deep

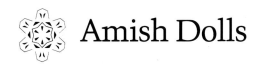

Amish Dolls

Amish dolls were almost always made without faces, since members of this religious sect considered it impious to make a human image. Our dolls are replicas of those made in the 1920's by mothers and grandmothers of children living in Wisconsin, Ohio, and Pennsylvania. They are dressed in typically plain, Amish costumes and include a rare boy doll.

Materials

For either doll:
1 pair of men's white cotton, tube socks.
Polyester stuffing.
Thread to match fabrics.

For girl doll:
Cotton fabrics: ⅜ yard rust orange,
⅜ yard black.
2 small hooks and eyes.

For boy doll:
Cotton fabrics: ¼-yard charcoal grey,
¼-yard light blue, 8" square black.
1 piece ⅜"-wide black, grosgrain ribbon.
Lightly-woven, straw placemat (for hat).
4 small hooks and eyes.
White glue.

To make either doll

Use a double strand of white thread to make a row of gathering stitches around one sock 3½" from toe; stuff the toe firmly to form the head. Draw the gathers to a diameter of 1" for neck; wrap thread around neck twice and knot tightly. Stuff next 7" of sock firmly to form a flat body; stitch across sock below stuffing by hand. Trim the sock 4¼" below stitching. Cut along the vertical center front and back of the leg section. Turn under ⅛" along edges of each leg and stitch fronts to backs; stuff firmly. From second sock, cut two 3½" by 6" arms. Fold each arm in half lengthwise and round off one end of each to form a hand. Turn under ⅛" along side and rounded edges; slip-stitch edges together. Sew arms to side of body ¾" below neck.

Since they have no features, the Amish dolls' personalities remain hidden, but a child can imagine what is behind those blank faces and might even draw a few lines with a crayon to show he or she understands.

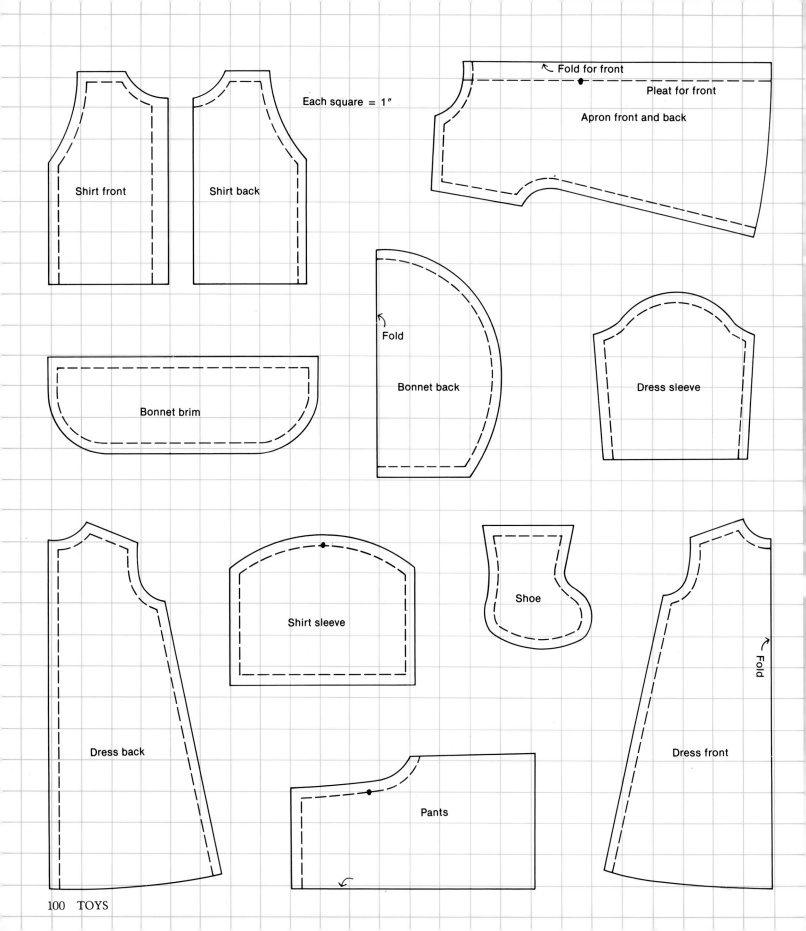

Each square = 1″

Shirt front

Shirt back

Fold for front

Pleat for front

Apron front and back

Fold

Bonnet back

Dress sleeve

Bonnet brim

Dress back

Shirt sleeve

Shoe

Fold

Dress front

Pants

A little Amish girl's new doll waits in the barn window while her mistress helps her grandmother shake out some quilts for an airing. The dark colors, blues and blacks and browns, are favored by "the plain people."

To make boy's hair

Wind yarn into a 13″ hank. Zigzag stitch across center of hank. Place yarn on doll's head centering stitching and slip-stitch in place. Clip and trim ends evenly.

To make boots

Cut 4 boots from black cotton fabric. With right sides in, stitch boot pieces together in pairs along curved edges. Turn under ¼″ along top edges. Stuff toes of boots; slip over ends of legs to 3¾″ below body. Slip-stitch along top edge.

To make girl's clothes

Cutting: from rust fabric, cut 1 dress front, 2 dress backs, 2 sleeves, and 1 collar strip 1¼″ × 5½″. From black fabric, cut 1 apron front, 2 apron backs, a 1¼″ × 7½″ bias strip for neck facing, 2 bonnet backs, 2 brims, two ties 1¼″ × 8″, and two ruffles 2″ × 7″.

The Dress: With right sides in, stitch backs together below dots; stitch backs to front along shoulders. Press seam allowance open above seam; stitch ⅛″ from fold. Press seams open. With right sides together, stitch collar strip to neck edge. Press collar away from dress; press under ¼″ on raw edges. Fold collar in half to inside; slip-stitch in place along seam. Stitch ⅛″ narrow hem along lower edges of sleeves. With right sides together, sew sleeves to dress. Stitch front to backs along side and sleeve seams. Narrow-hem lower edge of dress. Sew hook and eye to collar between center backs.

Bonnet: With right sides in, stitch brims together along curved edge; notch curves and turn right-side out. Turn under ¼″ along straight edge of bonnet back; gather curved edge between dots. With right sides together, pull gathers to fit and pin back to straight edge of brim. Stitch; machine-zigzag-stitch along seam allowance and press toward brim. Top-stitch ⅛″ from edges of brim. With right sides-in, fold ruffle in half lengthwise, and stitch ends. Clip corners and turn right-side out. Pleat ruffle to measure 2½″; baste along raw edge. Gather straight edge of back over ruffle and top stitch in place. Press under ¼″ on each long edge and one end of each tie; fold in half lengthwise. Stitch edges together. Sew a tie inside each side of base of brim.

Apron: On front, with rights sides out, stitch along pleat line from neck edge to dot. Match center front fold to seam line; press pleat. Stitch backs to front at shoulders. Fold bias strip in half; matching raw edges, stitch to neck edge. Clip seam allowance; press facing to wrong side. Top-stitch ⅛″ from neck edge. With right sides in, stitch front to backs along side seams. Make ¼″ double hem along lower edge. Sew hook and eye to top edges at center back.

To make boy's clothes

From gray, cut 2 pant legs, one 1¼″ by 11″ waistband, and two 1½″ by 9″ straps. From blue, cut shirt back, two sleeves, two fronts, two 1½″ by 4½″ cuffs and four 1½″ by 3¼″ bias-cut collars. From straw mat, cut one 5″ diameter circle and one 1″ by 10½″ crown strip.

Shirt: Press under ¼″, then ½″ along center front. Stitch ½″ from edge; then stitch ⅛″ from edge. Stitch fronts to back at shoulders. Stitch collars together in pairs, leaving one long edge open. Using ⅛″ seam, stitch collar to shirt at neck, matching sides of collar to center back and front and clipping collar and easing neck if necessary. Press seam toward shirt; top-stitch close to stitching. Press one long edge of cuff under ¼″. With right sides in, stitch raw edge of cuff to sleeve, making 3 small pleats at center of sleeve. Press seam toward cuff. Turn folded edge of cuff to inside, slip-stitch along stitching line. Stitch sleeve to shirt, matching dot to shoulder seam; stitch side and sleeve seams. Narrow-hem lower edge of shirt. Sew hook and eye at neck opening.

Pants: Fold pieces in half and stitch leg seam. Stitch crotch seam, leaving open on back above dot; Narrow-hem lower edge of each leg. Press under ¼″ on one long edge of waistband. Stitch waistband to wrong side of pants; press seams towards waist band. Fold waistband to right side and top-stitch in place. Turn center back edges to inside along seamlines and top-stitch. Sew snaps to center back at waistband. Press under ¼″ on long raw edges of straps; fold in half lengthwise so pressed edges meet and top-stitch. Top-stitch close to opposite edge. Top-stitch straps to inside of waistband ¾″ from center front. Put pants on doll; criss-cross straps in back and pin to waistband 1″ from center back and top-stitch in place.

Hat: Cut a 3″ circle from center of 5″ circle for hat top. With matching thread, make zigzag stitches around all edges of hat pieces to prevent fraying. Slip-stitch crown to brim stitching edges of crown together, and top to crown. Glue ribbon to base of crown.

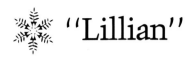

"Lillian"

"Lillian" sits for her formal portrait on an old, needlepoint-covered stool. We know she is more than 100 years old, but where she comes from is a mystery. Her self-assurance is unmistakable, however. The shawl "Lillian" has chosen to wear is a very old, handmade linen napkin with a pulled-work border; it was probably passed down from her grandmother. Realizing the importance of the occasion, she has applied just a hint of rouge to the tips of her toes.

"Lillian" is a most unusual doll. She is not a caricature, nor does she provoke laughter. She is, rather, an individual with a distinct personality who imprints herself on your memory like a beloved relative. Although a lovable animal, she has old-fashioned standards: She will speak sharply to a misbehaving child, but there's no doubt that her heart is a deep well of sympathy. "Lillian," in short, is a true lady (she remains seated at all times) and will be a true friend for life to any child who takes her in.

Materials

½ yard beige, cotton fabric.
Acrylic paints: white, black, and red.
Small paintbrush.
Polyester stuffing.
14" piece piping cord.
Thread: beige, pink, and off-white.
¼ yard pink, floral-print cotton.
⅝ yard bias tape.
2 sets snaps.
9" × 17" piece of off-white, linen fabric.
1 ⅜ yard ½" off-white lace.
¾ yard pink ribbon.

Our new "Lillian" prefers country ways and loves the outdoors. An exact copy of her 100-year-old namesake (except for the shawl), she has a twinkle in her painted eyes and a quiet dignity whose appeal seems to grow on both children and adults.

Cutting

Enlarge the patterns (see Skills Pages). For the doll, from beige fabric, cut: 2 head fronts, 2 head sides, 1 head back, 1 nose, 4 ears, 4 arms, 2 leg fronts, 2 leg backs, 2 upper fronts, 1 upper back, 1 lower back, and 1'' × 6½'' bias strip for tail. For the dress, from pink and white fabric, cut: 1 bodice front, 2 bodice backs, 2 sleeve strips 1½'' × 5½'', 2 skirt pieces 9'' × 11½'', and one pocket 1 ¾'' × 2''. Transfer markings for features to the right sides of head front and nose pieces. Transfer other markings to wrong side of pieces. Use ¼-inch seams.

Painting the features

If you're not adept at painting on fabric, try some of the features on scraps first. Then, on the head front, paint the eye area white and the pupil, eyebrow, and lash line black. Mix red and white paint to make pink and thin with water. Apply pink paint to center area of two ear pieces, to nose above mouth line, to cheek area, to tips of toe and hand areas, and to 2 arm pieces to make arm fronts. Allow pieces to dry. On nose area, paint nostrils and tongue red and mouth line black.

Making the head

For ears, sew painted ear fronts to other ear pieces along side edges. Clip curves and trim. Turn right side out. At lower edge, fold side seams to center, matching seam lines; baste. With painted side down, baste ears to right side of head front. With right sides together, stitch head side to head front. Stitch head-front pieces together along upper seam to dot and seam below nose. With right sides in, match dots and stitch head back to head fronts and sides. Turn under seam allowance on nose and nose seam of front. Stuff head firmly. Slipstitch nose to head.

Making the arms

With one painted arm in each pair, sew arms together in pairs, leaving short side open Clip curves; turn right side out. Stuff arms; baste open edges together on seamline.

Making the body

Clip seam allowance of upper edge of leg front at ½'' intervals. With right sides in, stitch leg fronts to upper front, matching dots. Stitch fronts together along center front, right sides in, from neck edge to second dot. Baste front of arms to right side of upper fronts between marks. With right sides in, stitch upper back to lower back along notched edge. Stitch darts in leg backs. With right sides in, stitch leg backs along center seam to dot. To make tail, fold bias strip around one end of piping cord. Starting at end, stitch along cord using a zipper foot; then stitch across cord. Trim seam allowance to ⅛'' from stitching. Turn cord right side out across end with stitching so cording covers other side of cord. Trim cord even with fabric on one end and slightly shorter on the other. Fold fabric under on end with shorter cord; slipstitch ends of fabric together. Tack tail into loop shape. Baste to top edge of right side of leg back over seam. Stitch leg backs to lower back, matching dots. With right sides together, stitch fronts to back, leaving neck edge open. Clip curves; turn right side out. Turn under seam allowance at neck edge and baste. Stuff legs and body. Pin head to neck edge of body, matching center front and back. Slipstitch head to body securely, pushing in as much stuffing as possible before closing seam.

Making the dress

With right sides in, stitch bodice front to back along shoulder seam. With right side in, stitch sleeve strips to armhole edge. Press under seam allowance on other long edge. Fold sleeve strip in half to wrong side; slipstitch to bodice along seam line. Fold ¼'' under twice along one 1¾'' edge of pocket; slipstitch hem in place. Press under ¼'' on remaining edge. Slipstitch pocket to one skirt piece 2¼'' from 11½'' top edge, and 2¼'' from side seam. Gather top edge to lower edge of bodice between sleeve strips. Slash skirt back along center back 3¼'' from top edge. Gather each side to bodice backs. Open one fold of bias tape. With right sides together, stitch bias tape to neck and center back seamlines. Clip curves along neck seam. Press bias tape to wrong side; slipstitch in place. With right sides together, stitch front to back along side seams. Turn up ¼'', and then 1¾'' along lower edge; slipstitch hem in place. Sew 2 snap sets between back bodice pieces. To make dress fabric look ''yellowed with age,'' wash fabric to remove sizing, and then soak dress in a bowl of strong tea for about 10 minutes. Rinse well and dry.

Making the hood

Press under ¼'' around edge of hood. Stitch lace over edge of hood, mitering at corners. Place hood over head. Pleat around neck; tie pink ribbon around neck with a bow in front.

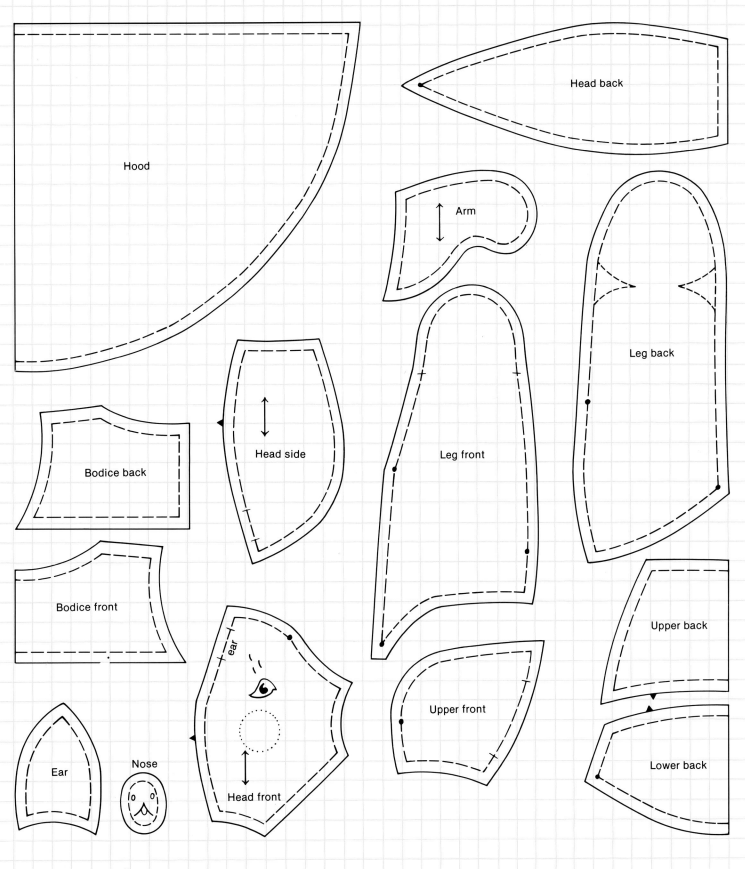

Hood

Head back

Arm

Leg back

Head side

Leg front

Bodice back

Bodice front

Leg front

Upper back

Upper front

Lower back

Ear

Nose

ear

Head front

Each square = ½"

Two bears prepare
for an outing in a late
nineteenth-century
wicker carriage. The
little vehicle has a pair
of iron safety wheels in
back to keep it from
tipping over backwards,
springs to soften the
ride, and a clever
handle that sets forward
to pull and folds
back for storage.

Two Bears

The original teddy bear was furry, of course, and complete directions for making "T.R. Bear," a traditional one, are given here. But bear dolls can be made more simply, as the instructions for the calico-patchwork bear prove. You can give either bear its own personality by paying close attention to its features; it is amazing how tightening the stitches to form the nose and eye sockets or giving a slightly different curve to the mouth can change a bear's looks.

T.R. Bear

Materials

½ yd 56"-wide brown, fake-fur fabric.
8" by 10" beige velveteen.
8" by 10" medium-weight, fusible interfacing.
Brown thread.
Brown or black carpet thread.
3 or 4 yds black, 3-ply Persian yarn.
Two ¾" black, shank buttons.
2 lbs. polyester stuffing.
T-pins.
5 2"-long cotter pins, ⅛" diameter (includes one extra for practice).
8 washers with hole smaller than cotter-pin head.
8 1½"-wide wooden discs, ⅛-in. thick, with ⅛" hole in center.
Awl or thin knitting needle.
Needle-nose pliers.

Cutting

Enlarge pattern pieces (See Skills Pages). Spread fake-fur fabric on work surface wrong-side-up, with nap of fur running down from top to bottom. Pin pattern pieces to wrong side of fabric. Cut out and transfer markings for the following: 1 each back, front, head side, inner arm, outer arm, inner leg, outer leg, head center, and two ears. Reverse pattern pieces and cut fabric pieces as before, except for head

center. From both interfacing and velveteen, cut one each sole and paw; reverse patterns and cut again from both materials.

Sewing hint: Smooth fur away from each edge of seam allowance with fingers, so fur will not catch in seam. If pile gets caught in seam, gently pull it out with a pin.

Making the body

With right sides together, stitch fronts to backs at side seams. Stitch pieces together along center seam. Turn under seam allowance on top edge and baste. Turn right-side out. With right sides together, stitch outer legs to inner legs, leaving an opening between notches at top and back. Fuse interfacing to wrong side of soles. Matching front

and back to corresponding seams on legs, pin and then stitch soles to legs. Turn right-side-out. Turn under seam allowance along opening and baste along edge.

Making the arms

Trim edge from paw interfacing along broken line. Fuse to wrong side of velveteen paws. Turn under seam allowance along interfacing; baste along edge. Pin in place on right side of inner arm, and using brown thread, slipstitch securely along hemmed edge. Baste along remaining seamline. With right sides together, stitch inner arms to outer arms leaving an opening between notches. Turn right-side-out. Turn under seam allowance along opening; baste along edges.

While on a hunting expedition out west, President Theodore Roosevelt spared the life of a cub bear whose mother had been slaughtered by the executive party. The newspapers picked up the story and made the little cub, nicknamed "Teddy" after the President, a national figure. Bear dolls appeared everywhere and to this day remain children's special favorites. This antique original is unusual because it is wearing a dress. Also, the fabric used for the torso of the body is the same plaid as the dress.

Attaching arms and legs

Make a practice joint using fabric first. Wooden discs should be held tightly together so that arms and legs will hold their position. Attach arms to upper dots and legs

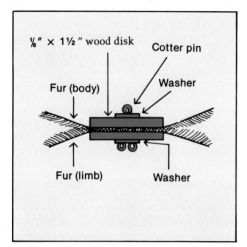

¹⁄₈ " × 1¹⁄₂ " wood disk   Cotter pin

Washer

Fur (body)

Fur (limb)   Washer

to lower dots. Slip a metal washer and then a wooden disc onto a cotter pin. With the awl or a knitting needle, make a hole the size of the cotter pin through each piece of fabric from the wrong side at the joint placement mark (large dot). Slip the cotter pin through the fabric of the body from the wrong side. Slip the cotter pin into the hole on the fur side of arm or leg. Slip a disc and then a washer onto the pin. Hold all the pieces together as tightly as possible while making a crown joint in this way: with the needle-nose pliers, grasp one leg of the cotter pin near the disc; bend it out and then down toward the center of the pin in a curve, so that the end is pressed against the washer. Repeat with the other limbs. Stuff the body, arms, and legs firmly. Pin openings on arms and legs together. Using carpet thread double in the needle, slipstitch edges together securely using very small stitches. To knot thread, sew a few small stitches in the same place; insert needle into fabric and bring up about 2 inches from knot. Clip ends of thread close to body.

Making the head

To mark positions for ears and eyes on the right side, using contrasting thread, make a stitch from fur side at position. Bring thread up to right side; tie ends together. Stitch darts in head side; slash dart along center line for about 1 " from edge. With right sides in, stitch head sides together along center front seam. Pin and then stitch head center to sides. Turn under seam allowance along neck edge and baste. Stuff head firmly. Pin

head to body, matching center front and back. Slipstitch head to body and knot securely. Embroider nose using black yarn and long, vertical straight stitches.

Making the mouth

Bring a 24 " length of yarn out at center front about ¼ " below nose. With T-pins mark positions for mouth: point 1 on center seam ½ " below nose; points 2 and 3 on head sides ¾ " below nose and 1½ " from center seam.

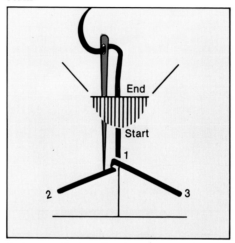

End

Start

1

2   3

Insert needle into head at point 2; bring it out at 1, leaving yarn slack. Run needle under and around the yarn and insert it at 3, bringing it out at top of nose. Remove pins. Pull yarn until mouth stitches lie flat. To knot, make a few stitches hidden among stitches of nose; clip thread close to nose.

Making the eyes

Thread a long needle with a double length of carpet thread. Insert needle into head at inside mark for ear and bring it out at eye mark on same side, leaving about 6" of thread extending from ear mark. Push awl into the fabric at eye next to thread to make a hole the size of the button shank. Remove thread mark. Slip needle through button shank and insert needle into hole, bringing up needle at ear. Remove needle from thread. Pull ends of double thread tight; tie several secure knots. Insert thread ends into needle and imbed ends in head.

Making the ears

With right sides together, stitch ears together in pairs, leaving shorter curve open. Turn right side out. Turn under seam allowance along opening; slipstitch edges together. Pin ears to position on head, curving ears slightly to front. Slipstitch ears securely to head.

T.R. Bear's Overalls

Materials

½ yd. blue, denim fabric.
Scrap of red bandana fabric.
Blue and red thread.
Two ½ " red buttons.

Cutting

If denim contains sizing, wash and dry it before cutting. Enlarge patterns (see Skills Pages). From denim, cut 2 fronts, 2 backs, 2 straps, and 1 pocket. From bandana, cut a 4½ " square.

Making the front

Note: use blue thread if not otherwise indicated. Use ¼ " seams.
With right sides together, stitch fronts together along center front seam. Press under ½ " on top edge of pocket; using red thread, stitch ¼ " from fold. Turn under ¼ " along remaining edges of pocket. Place pocket on left front as indicated; stitch along side and bottom edges.

Making the back

With right sides in, stitch backs together along center back seam.

Joining

Stitch front to back along side and inner leg seams. Zigzag or overcast stitch along longest edge of facing. With right sides in, stitch facing to top edge of front. Clip seams and corners; turn facing to wrong side. Turn under ¼ " along underarm and back edges. Topstitch ¹⁄₈ " hem along entire upper edge, using red thread.

Making the straps

Fold straps in half lengthwise with right sides in. Stitch seam along pointed end and long edge. Clip corners; turn right side out. Stitch ¹⁄₈ " from fold and finished end, using red thread. Make button hole at position indicated on strap, using blue thread. Sew straps under back edge at sides so that they cross in back.

Finishing

Turn under ¼ " and then ½ " along lower edge of overall legs. Topstitch hem using red thread. Sew buttons to front at positions indicated. Turn under ¼ " on bandana square; stitch ¹⁄₈ " from edge using red thread; insert in pocket.

T.R. Bear's Dress

Materials

¾ yd. pink-plaid fabric.
Sewing thread to match fabric.
½ yd. ¾″ eyelet ruffling.
4 sets of snaps.
Small piece of elastic.

Cutting

Using pattern pieces, from plaid fabric, cut 1 front with center on fold, 2 backs, and 2 sleeves. Also cut 1 skirt piece 7½″ by 40½″, and 1 bow 3½″ by 24½″. Transfer markings to fabric.

Making the bodice

Turn under ¼″ and then ½″ along center back edge of bodice backs; stitch along edge of hem. With right sides together, stitch backs to front at shoulder seams. Turn under ¼″ along neck edge; make a row of gathering stitches along edge. Gather area indicated along neck back to 2½″, and secure with pins. Cut length of elastic to fit neck edge plus 1″. Turn under ¼″ twice on ends for hem, and stitch in place. Place neck edge of bodice over inner edge of ruffling; stitch edges together.

Making the sleeves

Turn under ¼″ twice on lower edge of sleeve; stitch hem in place. Make a row of gathering stitches along seam line at top edge. With right sides together, gather sleeve to fit armhole edge of bodice; stitch seam. With right sides in, stitch front to backs along sleeve and side seams.

Making the skirt

Turn under ¼″ and then 1″ along one long edge for hem. Following diagram, mark measurements for pleats using pins. Fold pleats and press in place, holding them at top edge of skirt with a pin. Baste along top edge. Beginning 2½″ from top edge, stitch ends together, using a ½″ seam. Turn under ¼″ twice along edges above seam and stitch in place. With right sides in, stitch skirt to bodice.

Making the bow

Fold bow piece in half lengthwise. Measure 1½″ from ends and mark a line diagonally to the end at fold; trim ends along line. Stitch ¼″ from ends and long edge, leaving a 3″ opening in center for turning. Trim corners; turn right side out. Slipstitch edges together along opening. Tie a bow and sew to dress at center front below neck edge.

Finishing

Sew four sets of snaps between center back edges of bodice at positions indicated.

T.R. Bear, all dressed up in new denim overalls, strikes a confident pose as he awaits instructions for his part in the Christmas festivities.

Patchwork Bear

Materials

24″ by 48″ piece of an old quilt top or patchwork made from 3″ squares of assorted prints.
Scraps of print fabrics.
Scrap of solid red fabric.
Scrap of black felt.
2 flat, black buttons, ¾″ in diameter.
White and black thread.
Polyester stuffing.
1 yd. ¾″-wide grosgrain ribbon.

Cutting

Enlarge pattern pieces (see Skills Pages); pin to wrong sides of fabrics. From quilt top or patchwork fabric, cut 1 back, 1 front, 2 legs, and 2 head fronts. From print fabric, cut two snout pieces, and 4 ear pieces. From red fabric, cut 1 red heart. From black felt, cut 1 nose and 1 mouth.

Making the front

With right sides together, stitch head fronts together along short center edges. With right sides in, stitch snout together along center seam. With seams matched, stitch snout to head front. Stitch ear pieces together in pairs along curved edges. Clip curves; turn right side out. Topstitch ¼″ from curved edge. Baste to head front at position indicated. Stitch head front to front along neck edge.

Making the legs

With right sides in, fold legs in half, matching the edges; stitch, leaving the top edge open. Clip curves; turn right side out and stuff firmly. Fold front to back, matching the seam to the center fold. Baste along top seam line.

Making the back

Stitch darts in the back.

Making the body

Pin and stitch front to back, leaving the straight lower edge open. Clip curves; turn right side out. Baste legs to front at position indicated. Stuff arms to dotted line. Quilt along line. Stuff head and body firmly. Pin back to front at lower edge, turning under seam allowance; slipstitch edges together.

Making the features

Whipstitch nose and mouth to snout. Sew buttons to position indicated for eyes.

Finishing

Press under seam allowance on the heart. Place on left side of body with a small amount of stuffing under it. Slipstitch to body. Tie the ribbon around the bear's neck and make a bow.

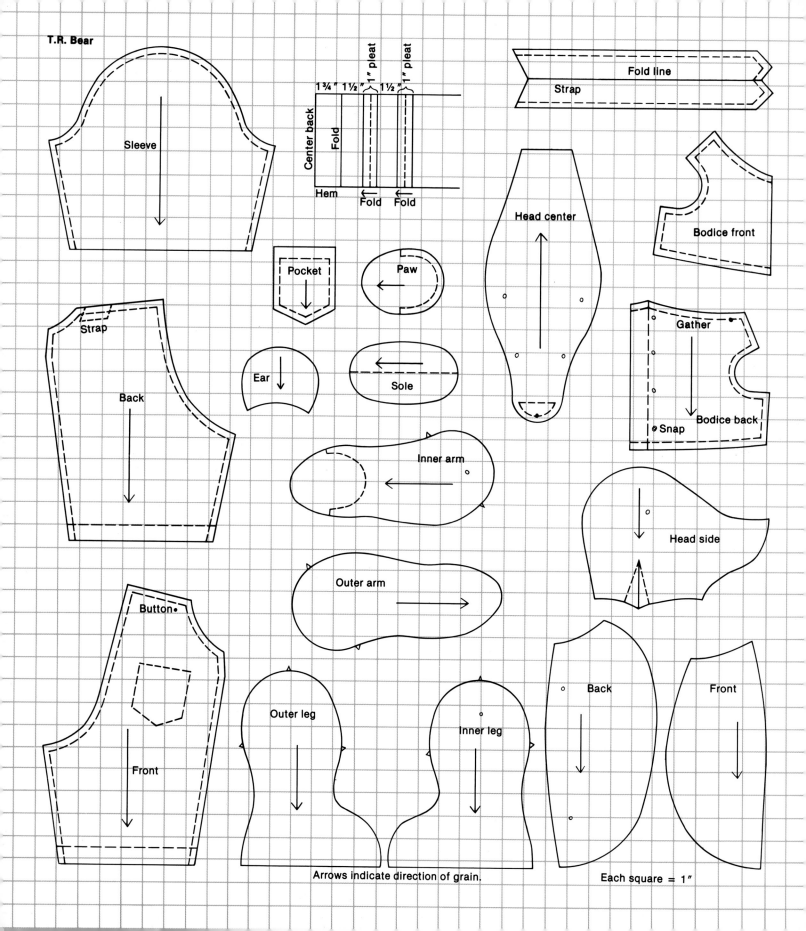

T.R. Bear

Sleeve

Center back
Fold
1¾" 1½" 1" pleat 1½" 1" pleat
Hem
Fold Fold

Fold line
Strap

Head center

Bodice front

Pocket

Paw

Strap

Back

Ear

Sole

Gather

Bodice back

Snap

Inner arm

Head side

Outer arm

Button•

Front

Outer leg

Inner leg

Back

Front

Arrows indicate direction of grain.

Each square = 1"

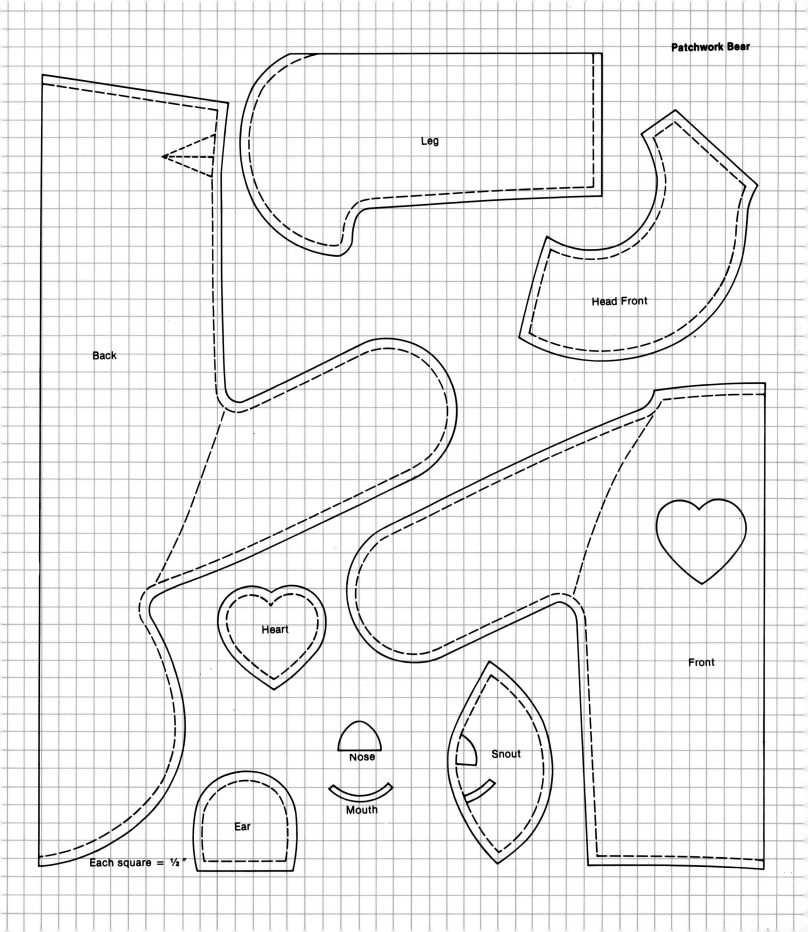

Patchwork Bear

Leg

Head Front

Back

Front

Heart

Heart

Nose

Snout

Mouth

Ear

Each square = ½"

Perhaps the most lasting appeal of old dolls is the individual personalities reflected in their faces. Their features may have been simply painted on, embroidered in delicate stitches, or formed with buttons, yet they charm their way into the hearts of their owners to become friends for life—sometimes for generations.

A soft, cuddly doll will keep little fingers busy learning how to fasten buttons (down the back), make hair bows, and tie shoe laces. Over the years she will become a beloved friend who will help recall memories of the happy holiday that marked her arrival.

Buttons-and-Bows Doll

Although this doll's stuffed body is easy to make, her colonial-print dress that is gathered across the bodice, bloomers with white eyelet trim, yarn hair-bows, and colorful ballet-slipper laces give her an old-new fashioned look that will turn heads and warm hearts. Before you buy new fabric, check your sewing chest for remnants, since the amount needed is minimal. You can determine how much you need after enlarging the pattern pieces onto tissue paper. (See Skills Pages.)

Materials and tools

Fabric: ¼ yd. unbleached muslin. Remnants of calico or small-print cotton; dark-colored heavy canvas or duck; white cotton. Thread to match fabric.
3½ yds. of lace trim, 1″ wide.
2′ of plaid ribbon, 1″-wide.
27″-long plaid shoelaces.
Fiberfill or shredded rags.
Light-colored tracing paper.
Tracing wheel.

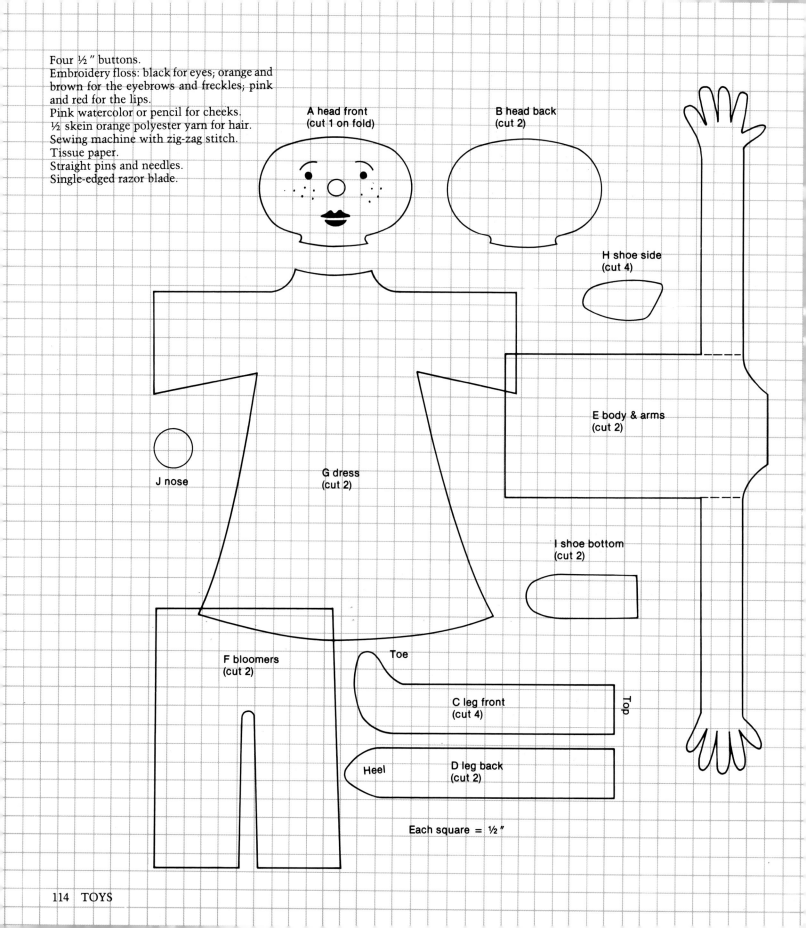

Four ½" buttons.
Embroidery floss: black for eyes; orange and brown for the eyebrows and freckles; pink and red for the lips.
Pink watercolor or pencil for cheeks.
½ skein orange polyester yarn for hair.
Sewing machine with zig-zag stitch.
Tissue paper.
Straight pins and needles.
Single-edged razor blade.

A head front
(cut 1 on fold)

B head back
(cut 2)

H shoe side
(cut 4)

E body & arms
(cut 2)

J nose

G dress
(cut 2)

I shoe bottom
(cut 2)

F bloomers
(cut 2)

Toe

C leg front
(cut 4)

Top

Heel

D leg back
(cut 2)

Each square = ½"

Front seam

Front hairline should not exceed ½" beyond front seam of face.

Middle seam or part

Insert needle and yarn ¼" away from middle seam; pull out as close to seam as possible. Pull strand ends until they are even.

Before you begin to sew

1. Enlarge all pattern pieces from grid onto tissue paper. From muslin, cut out head, body and legs; from calico, dress; from white cotton, bloomers; from canvas, shoe pieces. Add ¼" seam allowance to all pieces.
2. Trace all markings from pieces onto *wrong* side of fabric *except* for facial features, which should be traced onto the right side.
3. Iron edge of nose piece J under and gather with running stitch. Stuff with fiberfill, then close up by sewing a few hand stitches.
4. Attach nose to center of front head piece A stitching *securely* by hand.
5. With embroidery thread, put on the facial features using the markings as a guide to their placement.
6. Paint on cheeks using watercolor or colored pencil, taking care not to smudge.

Making the hair

1. Cut orange yarn into 16 in. pieces.
2. Thread a needle with the yarn and insert it ½ in. up from base of doll's neck. Use head's center seam as a guide to where the hair part will be.
3. Insert needle ¼ in. away from middle seam and pull it out as close to seam as possible. Pull one end of the strand out until it is even with other end.
4. Repeat Steps 2 and 3 for each side of the hair part, one side at a time. The front hairline should end ½ in. beyond the front seam of the doll's face.
5. Begin to braid the yarn below the ear level, close to the sides of the face.
6. With yarn and needle, tack braids to each side of the head, just below the "ears."
7. Cut the plaid ribbon into two 1-ft. pieces, and tie into bows around each braid.

Making the bloomers

1. Sew inner leg and side seams of bloomer piece F. Iron under the waist ¼ in., then turn under another ¼ in. Stitch.

2. Hem bloomers and sew lace trim around the inside of each edge.

Making the head

1. Right sides together, pin, then stitch center seam of back head piece B.
2. Pin, then stitch side seams of front head A to back head B, right sides together, matching center of face with back piece's center seam.
3. Turn head right-side-out and stuff, leaving the neck open.

Making the legs

1. Right sides together, pin and stitch center seam of front leg piece C, stopping at tip of toe.
2. Stitch back leg pieces D to front leg pieces C, beginning at tip of toe, matching seam with center of the toe on piece D. Stitch side seams.
3. Turn legs right-side-out and stuff, leaving ½ in. from the top unfilled. Close off each leg by stitching across the upper edges.

Making the arms and upper body

1. Stitch side seams of body and arm piece E, including the fingers and arms. *Do not* stitch neck or leg openings or inner-leg area.
2. Slash fabric between fingers, close to the stitchline.
3. Turn right-side-out, using a knitting needle for easier turning of the fingers.
4. Stuff only the arms.
5. Stitch along line from underarm to top of arm at the shoulder.
6. Attach head by inserting the neck inside body piece E. Slip-stitch around neck to secure it firmly to head.
7. Stuff head solidly until it stands upright without drooping. Stuff the rest of body *except* the leg openings.
8. Sew inner-leg seam. Fold under ¼ in. inside each opening.
9. Attach legs to body by inserting their top edges into body's openings; sew a running stitch straight across, through all four thicknesses.

Making the dress

1. Take one of dress pieces G and cut down center line, making two sections.
2. Right sides together, pin and stitch pieces to each other under the arms and at each shoulder.
3. Cut from the calico a strip 1-in. wide, 28 in. long, for a seam binding, which will finish the raw edges of the dress's back opening and neckline. Iron under ¼ in. on each side of the binding; fold in half and iron wrong sides together.
4. Starting at bottom of dress, pin raw edge up inside the folded edges of the binding along one back opening, around neck edge, and down the other side of the opening; top stitch.
5. Make dress belt by cutting a piece of fabric 2 in. wide and 36 in. long. Fold piece in half and stitch raw edges together. Turn right-side-out and iron belt out flat so the seam is now in the middle of one side of the flattened belt.
6. Cut one yard of lace trimming in half and stitch the raw edges together. Place the lace against the seamed side of the belt and topstitch the edges so that the lace forms borders on both sides of the belt.
7. Make a hem ¼ in. deep along bottom of dress and edge of each sleeve. Sew lace around each hem; topstitch.
8. Make four button holes down the back at even intervals. Sew on buttons.

Making the shoes

1. With right sides together, seam two shoe sides together along the top, from the toe 1½" up. Press seam open.
2. With right sides together, pin and then stitch sides to bottom, starting at toe and going up the back. Turn right side out.
3. Turn in raw edge at back of shoe and hem.
4. Cut two holes on each side of shoe opening for laces. Put in metal eyelets, or finish as button holes.
5. Repeat for second shoe; slip shoes on doll's feet and lace up.

This walnut Chippendale baby cradle was made in Pennsylvania around 1800. The two hand holes at the sides are obviously for lifting the cradle, but the two porcelain knobs are somewhat puzzling: perhaps they were used to tie baby and coverlet safely in.

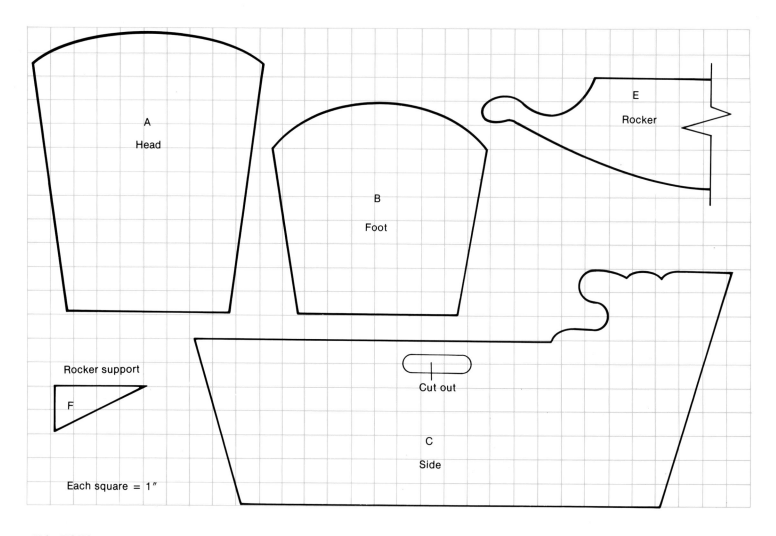

A
Head

B
Foot

E
Rocker

Rocker support

F

Cut out

C

Side

Each square = 1″

Colonial Doll Cradle

This cradle is a scaled-down replica of an eighteenth-century rocking cradle; the original was made for a baby, but this one is intended to rock a sleepy doll.

To ensure that each piece fits properly, when assembling the cradle, first use as few nails as possible, driving them only deep enough to hold the pieces together. When you are satisfied with the fit, reassemble the parts with glue and with nails driven home and countersunk.

Materials

Pine lumber, ½" thick. See materials chart for size and quantity.
½ lb. of ¾" finishing nails.
Wood glue.
Sandpaper, 2 sheets each of medium and fine grades.
Wood filler (optional).
Stain and varnish (optional).
Paint (optional); make sure it's non-toxic.

Tools

Sabre or coping saw.
Ruler.
Hammer.

Preparing the pieces

1. Enlarge the pieces from the grid; draw designs onto the side pieces (C), using the pattern as a guide and cut out.

2. Sand each piece, first with the medium, then with the fine-grade sandpaper.
3. Before gluing any of the pieces together, make sure they fit properly. Refer to figure for all assemblies.

Assembling the cradle

1. Nail cradle head (A) and foot (B) between the sides (C).
2. Temporarily attach the rocker pieces (E) to cradle bottom (H). Make sure the cradle rocks evenly before gluing.
3. Nail and glue the rocker support pieces (F) to the rockers.
4. Use glue and nails to attach the top of the cradle to the bottom. Nail through the bottom assembly into the raw edges of the top.

Finishing

1. Carefully sand the cradle to remove all sharp edges and splinters.
2. Countersink all nails. Fill holes. Sand and finish with wood filler (optional), stain, and varnish.

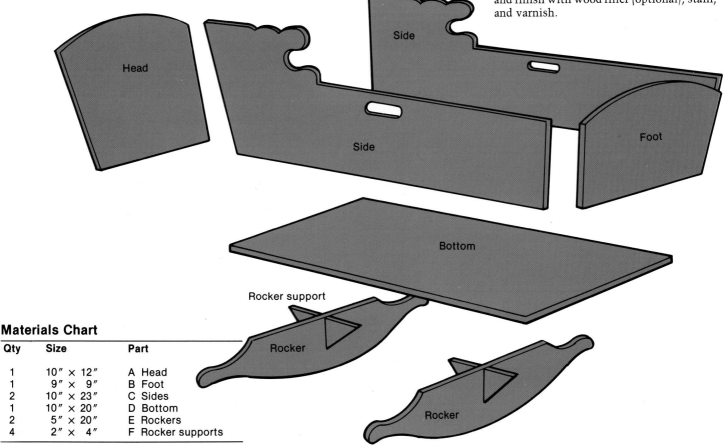

Materials Chart

Qty	Size	Part
1	10" × 12"	A Head
1	9" × 9"	B Foot
2	10" × 23"	C Sides
1	10" × 20"	D Bottom
2	5" × 20"	E Rockers
4	2" × 4"	F Rocker supports

❄ Cradle Coverlet

The design pictured here adapts the five-petal flower motif of the print, but any small-scale print and appropriate design will work. If you choose pastels, rather than the bright colors shown, select the print first and then buy three complementary colors to combine with it. The finished size is 25 by 33 inches.

The old quilt beneath the doll in the cradle is made in the "Grand-mother's Flower Garden" design, a traditional English pattern. Like the coverlet, it consists of many multi-sided pieces of cloth. But the quilt is "pieced" together—all the hexagonal sections are sewn to each other; while the coverlet is "appliqued"—all the design elements are sewn to a single, large piece of cloth.

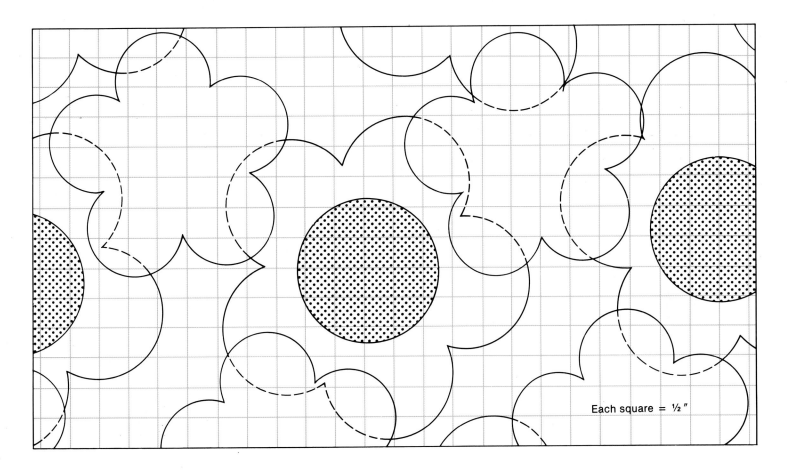

Each square = ½"

Materials

36"-wide cotton fabric:
1¼ yds. of the desired print
¾ yds. of solid white
⅜ yd. each of red, rose, and orange or the colors of your choice.
¾ yd. of blanketing or quilted fabric for the interlining (a good section of an old blanket will do).
Sewing thread to match all fabric, including the background color of your print.

Tools

Sewing needle and pins.
Scissors.
Tracing paper.
Cardboard.
Ruler.

Cutting the fabric

1. Cut a 32-in. × 40-in. rectangle out of the print fabric. This one piece will serve as the back of the coverlet, as well as the print border on the front.
2. Cut a 25-in. × 33-in. rectangle out of the white cotton fabric for the background of the appliqué.

3. Cut a 25-in. × 33-in. rectangle out of the blanket or quilted fabric for the interlining.

Preparing to appliqué

1. Enlarge the patterns to full-size (see Skills Pages for instructions) and cut cardboard patterns for the flowers and flower center (or for the design of your choice).
2. Cut out the following pieces, adding ¼-in. allowances for the seams: 7 orange and 8 rose pieces from the large flower pattern; 19 red pieces from the small flower pattern; 15 centers from the print fabric.
3. Extend the full-sized pattern to 25" × 33". Center the pattern on the white background fabric and transfer it to the fabric.
4. Press the seam allowances to the wrong side on all the appliqué pieces, clipping and slashing as necessary (see Skills Pages for instructions).

To appliqué the pieces

1. Baste one center in place on each large flower. Then appliqué, using the blind method (see Skills Pages.)
2. Baste the large flowers in place on the white fabric, using the photograph as a

guide if you are using the same design and color arrangement. Blind appliqué the large flowers to the background, and then baste and appliqué the small red flowers in place.

Finishing

1. Put the print backing right-side-down on a table and center the interlining fabric on the wrong side of it.
2. Pin and baste carefully from the center out, then stitch around the edges of the interlining.
3. Place the appliqued white fabric face up on the interlining and pin and baste it to the interlining.
4. Fold the print edges over the right side of the coverlet. Miter the corners (see Skills Pages).
5. Turn the raw edges in ½ in. and blindstitch the print to the right side of the coverlet. Make sure that the stitches do not go through to the back of the coverlet. Next, blindstitch each mitered corner.
6. You can work a few stitches through the print centers of the flowers all the way to the back of the coverlet. This will hold the interlining securely in place.

The design of this rocking horse is similar to many that were made in the nineteenth century. This one is unusual because its pieces are hand-carved, rather than turned. The mortise-and-tenon construction with square pegs dates the toy to around 1830.

Here is the familiar hobby horse in a menacing guise: new members of a fraternal order in upstate New York rode this hazing goat in the late nineteenth century during their initiation ritual. The strongest member of the order pulled and pushed the rear handle violently in an attempt to dislodge the inductee from his leather-covered, horsehair-stuffed mount.

Old-Fashioned Rocking Horse

You can make an heirloom rocking horse much like a design first made in 1850 and now on display at the Ford Museum. This project can be done in a weekend and is a delightful, longlasting toy your children will enjoy, from toddler to six-year-old.

Materials and tools

About 1½ 4 × 8 sheets of ¾" plywood.
About 5' of wooden dowel rod, 1" in diameter.
Finishing nails, 1½" long.
8 wood screws, 1½" long.
Carpenter's wood glue.
One 11" × 17" piece of leather, canvas, or upholstery fabric.
Staple gun and staples, or small tacks and a tack hammer.

One 10" × 16" piece of 2"-thick foam rubber.
2 yds. of decorative upholstery tape.
Decorative upholstery tacks.
Ruler and pencil.
Sabre saw, screwdriver, sandpaper.
Electric drill with 1" spade bit and ³⁄₃₂" bit.
Router with corner-round bit (optional).

Cutting and preparing the pieces

1. Enlarge the pattern pieces from the grid (see the Skills Pages for instructions), and transfer them to plywood.
2. Use a sabre saw to cut out all the pieces. Do not cut the bottom angle of the head pieces until time to attach them to the seat.
3. Glue and nail the two head pieces together. Rout both edges of the top and sides of the head if you wish.
4. Smooth the edges of all pieces with sandpaper.

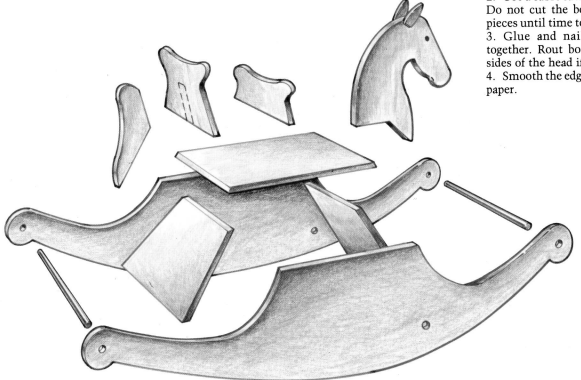

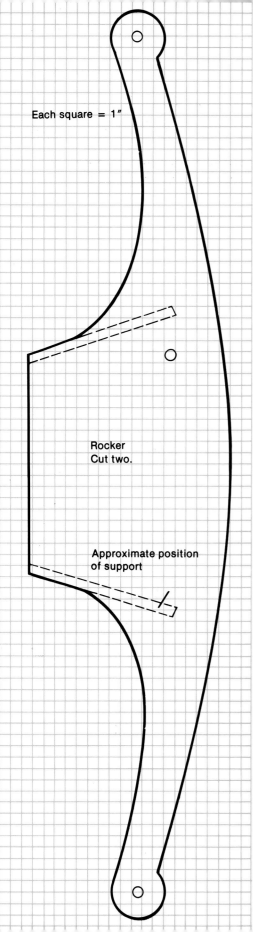

Each square = 1″

Rocker
Cut two.

Approximate position
of support

Every child dreams of having a real, live pony, and every parent (except for those who live on farms and ranches) winces at the thought. But a little imagination and ingenuity can go a long way toward making a dream come partly true. Most young children will happily settle for an old-fashioned, wooden rocking horse.

Assembling the pieces

TIP: If you use glue along with the nails and screws, this steed will be around for the grandchildren, too.

1. Temporarily assemble the rockers and the rocker supports, lightly nailing them together. Set the tops of the supports flush with the top corners of the rockers; the position is indicated on the rocker pattern.
2. Place the assembly on a level floor to check the rocking action; adjust the positions of the pieces. When the action is smooth and even, remove the nails and permanently fasten the rockers to the supports with glue and wood screws.
3. Insert dowels through the front and back holes in the rockers; cut them flush with the outside of the rocker. The footrest dowel should pass through both rockers with about 5 inches extending on each side. Fasten all dowels with finishing nails and glue.
4. Before assembling the top pieces, trim the front of the seat to match the angle where it meets the front-rocker support; do the same in back. Trim the bottom of the backrest so that it will lean slightly backwards when attached to the seat.
5. Cut the bottom angle of the head to fit the angle of the seat and front support. Nail and glue the two ears to the head.
6. Attach the head, backrest, and saddlehorn to the seat with two screws each. (Be sure the screws for the backrest are driven at an angle.) The saddlehorn fits flush with the back of the head; drive one screw through the saddlehorn into the head.
7. For extra lateral support for the head, cut two wooden blocks and fasten them with nails and glue on both sides at the base of the head.

Final assembly

Place the top assembly over the rocker assembly and fasten them together with glue and nails or screws driven through the top of the seat. If you use screws, countersink them to avoid scratching the rider. Fill nail or screw holes with wood filler.

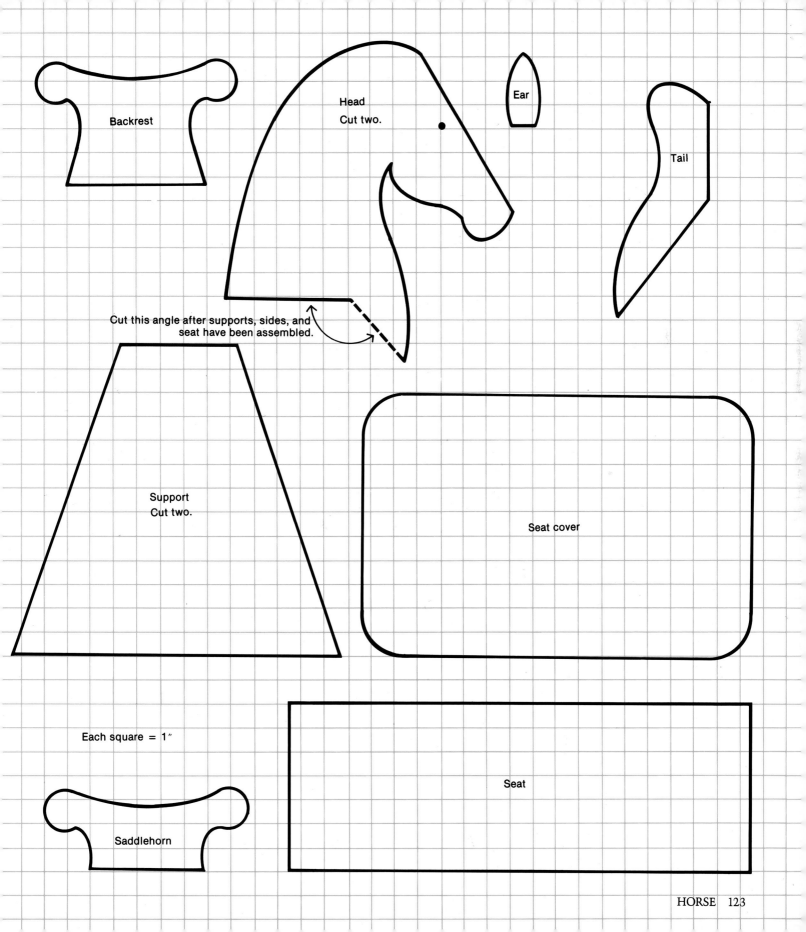

Backrest

Head
Cut two.

Ear

Tail

Cut this angle after supports, sides, and
seat have been assembled.

Support
Cut two.

Seat cover

Each square = 1″

Saddlehorn

Seat

The handsome nineteenth-century rabbit (above) was designed for very un-rabbit-like behavior: two pieces of heavy cast iron were bolted together to act as a door stop. The little creature at right is actually a beaver, carved from a single piece of heavy walnut. He'll hold a door, too, if you push his tail underneath.

❊ Peter Rabbit Pull-Toy

The front wheel (the paws) of this pull-toy is mounted off-center, so that Peter Rabbit bobs as he rolls along. Years ago the wheel would have been metal, probably cast iron; but few home workshops are equipped for that kind of work today. You might try "shoeing" the wheel: cut a strip of tin from the right-sized can, solder it tight around the wheel, file it smooth, and then tack it to the wood with small, flat-headed wire nails. To make the nails look like old-fashioned hand-made ones, square off their round heads with a grinding wheel or a file.

This sturdy pine pull-toy is built to last, and after you've made one, you'll probably be asked to make another and another—enough to fill a rabbit hutch. You can paint it if you like, using non-toxic paint, of course, but it really isn't necessary. The grain of the wood gives the bunny a beautiful, natural decoration of its own.

Materials

2' of molding strip, ½" × 4".
1' clear pine plank, 2 × 8.
6"-length of ⅜" dowel.
2 round wooden toothpicks.
4 wood screws, ¾" no. 6 (flat heads).
2 brass wood screws, 1" no. 8 (flat heads).
2 flat washers, ½", with ⅛" hole.

Tools

Electric drill with the following bits: $\frac{3}{32}$", ⅛", ¼", ⅜".
Sabre or coping saw with 3" scroll sabre-saw blade.
Sandpaper.
NON-TOXIC clear wood finish.

Instructions

1. Trace outline of shapes onto wood, making sure that the ear lengths are parallel to the grain of the plank.
2. With coping or sabre saw, using a 3-in. fine or medium scroll blade, cut out shapes.
3. Sand all shapes, rounding the edges and smoothing out the saw-blade marks until you are satisfied with the degree of smoothness.
4. Mark and drill all pieces according to instructions on the pattern.
5. Attach small wheels to the rear legs with brass screws, putting washer between wheel and leg on each side.
6. Insert one 2-in. dowel into holes on the insides of rear legs.
7. Align holes in rear legs with pilot holes on body and attach with ¾-in. no. 6 wood screws.
8. Put front axle dowel (with $\frac{3}{32}$-in. holes drilled as per pattern instructions) into electric drill. Run drill and hold sandpaper against dowel area between holes (so front wheel will turn freely).
9. Mount front wheel on axle between holes, inserting ¾-in. pegs cut from centers of two round toothpicks.
10. Insert front axle into holes on front legs.
11. Align holes in front legs with pilot holes on body and mark proper angle for attaching front legs to body.
12. Put glue on body where front legs will cover, align holes and angle markings, and attach front legs to body with ¾-in. no. 6 wood screws.
13. Screw the screw-eye into the centered pilot hole as shown.
14. Cut 4¼-in. plugs out of $\frac{5}{16}$-in. dowel; glue into the countersunk holes on the legs. Sand flush when dry.

If Mr. MacGregor turns around, it's all over for Peter Rabbit this time! The menacing gardener is made of pieces of 2 × 12 cut with a band saw and glued together. The arms and legs are hinged with through-bolts at elbow and knee, and they swing on lag-bolts with washers at shoulder and hip. The big, flat feet are glued to the legs at right angles. He stands, bends, sits, and makes the biggest dress-up doll in the county.

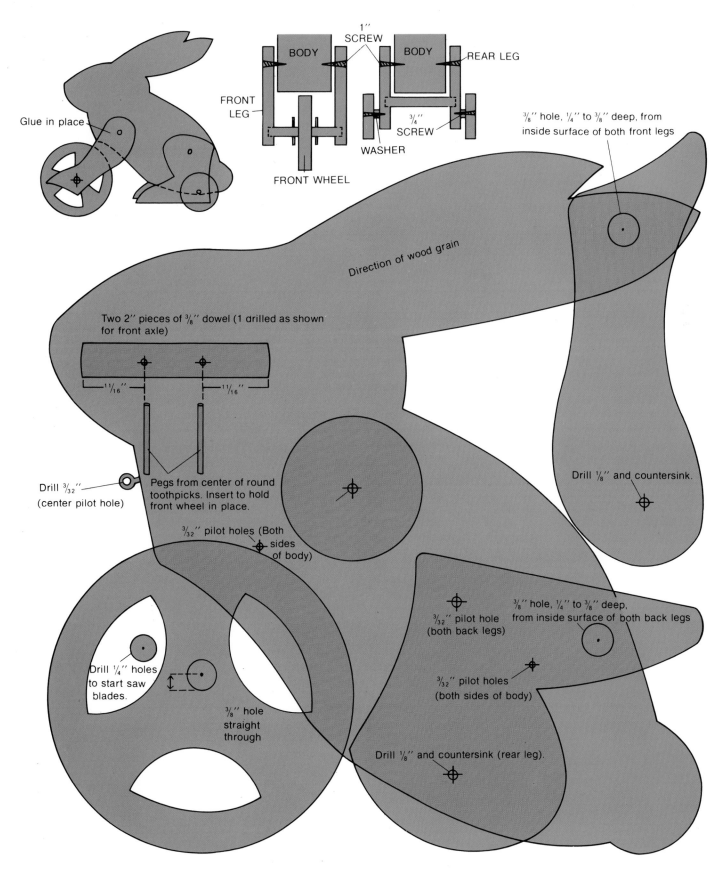

Glue in place

1" SCREW

BODY

BODY

REAR LEG

FRONT LEG

³⁄₄" SCREW

WASHER

FRONT WHEEL

³⁄₈" hole, ¹⁄₄" to ³⁄₈" deep, from inside surface of both front legs

Direction of wood grain

Two 2" pieces of ³⁄₈" dowel (1 drilled as shown for front axle)

1¹⁄₁₆"

1¹⁄₁₆"

Drill ³⁄₃₂" (center pilot hole)

Pegs from center of round toothpicks. Insert to hold front wheel in place.

Drill ¹⁄₈" and countersink.

³⁄₃₂" pilot holes (Both sides of body)

³⁄₈" hole, ¹⁄₄" to ³⁄₈" deep, from inside surface of both back legs

³⁄₃₂" pilot hole (both back legs)

³⁄₃₂" pilot holes (both sides of body)

Drill ¹⁄₄" holes to start saw blades.

³⁄₈" hole straight through

Drill ¹⁄₈" and countersink (rear leg).

❄ North-Pole Biplane

Although Santa himself always travels by sled, his helpers often use faster transportation to make sure that every child receives gifts on time. Back in the 1920's, a speedy biplane was the most reliable craft in Santa's airforce; this sturdy model will surely make a child's eyes light up with delight.

These early twentieth-century model airplanes are fanciful creations made in the typical American folk-art spirit. The biplane (below) is constructed of polychromed wood, and its pieces are bound together with baling wire. The tin plane on top was ingeniously made out of a sewer-pipe reamer and an oxygen cylinder, in the same whimsical spirit as Picasso's bull's head, made from a bicycle seat and handlebars.

Materials

Lumber and dowels: consult chart.
Sabre saw.
Wood rasp.
Drill with ¼ " and ½ " bits.
Sandpaper, both medium and fine grades.
Wood glue.
1" and 2" finishing nails.
Hammer.
3 metal washers

Cutting and shaping

1. Cut the pieces according to the patterns from the lumber specified in the chart.
2. Drill all holes where indicated by an X; make sure the holes are the same size as the corresponding dowels.
3. Shape and size the plane's body, nose-cone, and propeller with the wood rasp, according to the patterns, the finished drawing, and the photograph.
4. Thoroughly sand all the pieces of wood with medium- and then fine-grain sandpaper.

Assembling the plane

1. Nail and glue the thick wheel support to the center of the lower wing, as indicated by the dotted lines on the pattern.
2. Nail and glue the lower wing to the body of the plane.
3. Wipe glue on the dowel wing support ends and insert into drilled holes in both wings. Set body and wing assembly aside to dry.
4. Glue and nail tail sections together; when dry, glue to rear of body.
5. Wipe glue on end of dowel and insert it through propeller, washer, nosecone, and into hole in front of body. Trim off excess dowel and glue slice of larger dowel to end to secure propeller.
6. Insert axle dowel through axle hole in wheel support; slip washers over both ends of axle; attach wheels to axle ends with a spot of glue.
7. Wipe glue on end of skid and insert in hole at rear of body.

Finishing

If you wish the plane to have a natural wood finish, varnish it. If you paint it, be sure to use non-toxic paint.

A child's imagination will take wing in this old biplane. You can paint the model in favorite colors and add Santa's image, if you wish, before the plane makes its appointed landing under the Christmas tree.

Lumber Chart

Qty	Description	Type of lumber
2	Wheels	½″ pine or plywood
1	Vertical tail	½″ pine or plywood
1	Horizontal tail	½″ pine or plywood
1	Upper wing	½″ pine or plywood
1	Lower wing	½″ pine or plywood
1	Propeller	½″ pine or plywood
1	Wheel support	2 × 4
1	Body	2 × 4
1	Nosecone	2 × 4
1	Axle	¼″ dowel, about 2¾″ long
1	Skid	¼″ dowel, about 1¼″ long
1	Propeller stop	¼″ dowel, about 2¾″ long
4	Wing supports	½″ dowel, 4½″ long
1	Pilot's neck	½″ dowel, about 1½″ long
1	Pilot's head	drawer pull or round finial, about 1″
3	Metal washers	with 5⁄16″ hole for ¼″ dowel

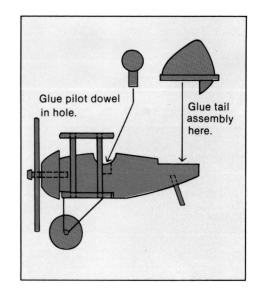

Glue pilot dowel in hole.

Glue tail assembly here.

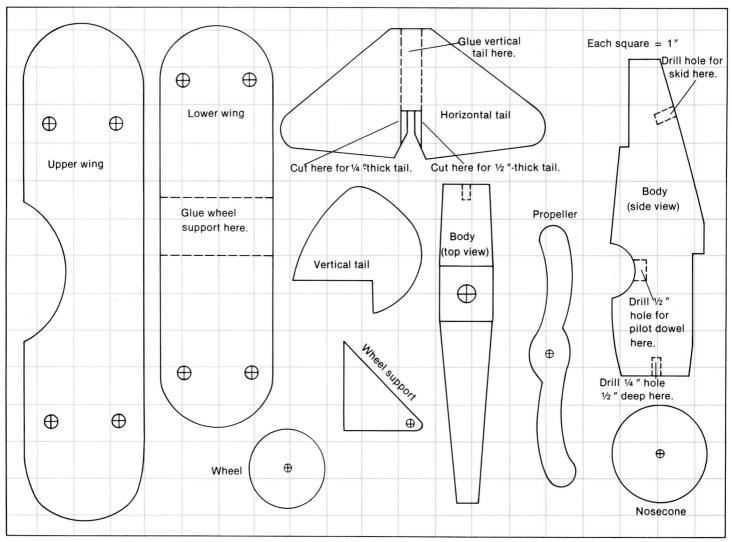

Glue vertical tail here.

Each square = 1″

Drill hole for skid here.

Horizontal tail

Cut here for ¼″-thick tail.

Cut here for ½″-thick tail.

Lower wing

Upper wing

Glue wheel support here.

Body (side view)

Vertical tail

Body (top view)

Propeller

Drill ½″ hole for pilot dowel here.

Wheel support

Drill ¼″ hole ½″ deep here.

Wheel

Nosecone

Little Blue Barrow

Anyone who enjoys making precise models will find this little wagon a pleasure to make. The more careful your workmanship, the closer the result will be in spirit to an old-time handmade barrow. The dusty blue color comes from the old-fashioned milk-based paint used.

This miniature wheelbarrow, a copy right down to its neat stake sides, makes a perfect conveyance for pinecones, fruits, candies, gifts—anything that brightens up the home at holiday time—if you are able to get it away from the children.

Materials and Tools

10" length of 1 × 6 pine
6½" × 8" piece ½" pine
2" × 20" strip ½" pine.
3½" × 36" piece ¼" pine.
Tin can with smooth (not corrugated) sides.
¾" nails (with heads).
1¼" nails (with heads).
½" brads (no heads).
Carpenter's wood glue.
Sandpaper.
Saber saw with fine scroll-cutting blade.
Tin snips or heavy utility shears.
Drill with ⅛" bit.
Hammer.
Compass.

Cutting the pieces

Cut the following pieces of wood and label them with pencil.
From ¼" pine:
One front—3⅜" × 4"
One back panel—2⅞" × 5¾"
Two side panels—2⅞" × 7¼"
Six panel braces—½" × 3⅜"
One leg brace—⅝" × 6"

From ½" pine:
One bottom—a trapezoid with a long base of 6⅜", a short base of 4", and a vertical height between the bases of 7⅜" (See Figure A).
Two handles—⅝" by 19½"

From ¾" pine:
One wheel—4¼" diameter
Two legs—¾" square by 2¾".

Assembling the barrow

1. Sand off any saw marks and sharp edges; round the corners on one end of each of the six side-panel braces.
2. Cut a wedge from the front end of each handle as shown in Figure B. Drill axle holes in the ends of the handles (Figure F).
3. Drill a ⅛" hole through the center of the wheel.
4. Cut six ½" × 2" strips of metal from a tin can. Follow steps shown in Figures C and D to form the panel brackets.
5. Draw straight vertical lines 1½" in from each end of the side panels, and 1" in from each end of the back panel. Using glue and ½-in. brads, attach the panel braces inside the lines as shown in Figure E.
6. Fasten one leg to each corner of the long end of the wheelbarrow bottom using 1¼-in. nails and glue.
7. Attach the leg brace between the legs 1" up from the bottom with ¾" nails and glue.
8. Fasten the handles to the bottom with ¾" nails and glue as shown in Figure F.
9. Mount the wheel, using a cut-off nail for an axle.
10. Fasten the front-end panel to the front of the bottom using ¾" nails and glue.
11. Hold side and back panels in place on the wheelbarrow to test for fit. Angle the edge of the panels to fit correctly using a fine wood rasp or coarse sandpaper on a block.
12. Hold panels in place one at a time and place brackets over the side braces, nailing them onto the sides of the bottom with ¾" nails.
13. Paint the wheelbarrow, leaving the brackets unpainted. The one shown was painted with an old-fashioned ''milk'' paint. (See box on milk paint in directions for ''Little Red Sled.'')

There was a time when the self-reliant made everything they could for themselves. A farmer would make, among other things, a peg rake from wood he grew, cut, and shaped himself. He would also make a wheelbarrow with stake sides that could be lifted off to accommodate extra-large loads. The flat-crowned Amish hat, however, was probably store-boughten.

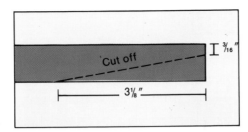

Figure B. Front of handle.

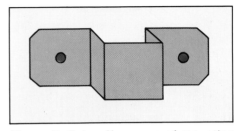

Figure D. Snip off corners of mounting brackets and punch holes in ends.

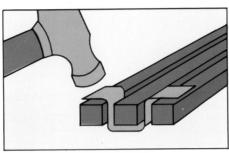

Figure C. Shape ½″ metal strips into mounting brackets by bending them around three panel braces and tapping with hammer.

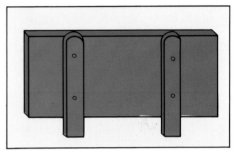

Figure E. Attach panel braces to panels 1½″ from ends on side panels and 1″ from ends on back panel, leaving ½″ extending below panel.

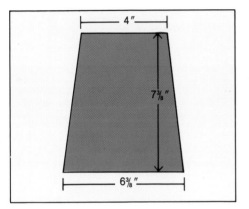

Figure A. Bottom of wagon.

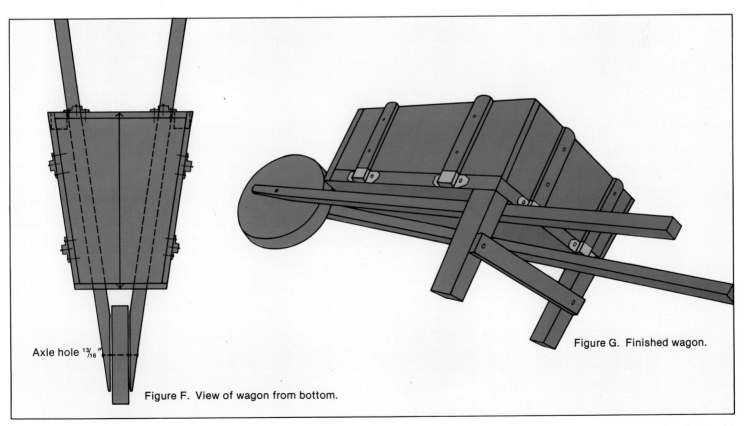

Axle hole ¹³/₁₆″

Figure F. View of wagon from bottom.

Figure G. Finished wagon.

This little red sled is just the right size to carry a teddy bear or a pair of gloves, suitably wrapped, on their journey to the family's Christmas tree. (Flour makes good snow if you can't find the plastic kind in a bag. Both require vacuuming to clean up.)

Just as the old-fashioned sleigh led inevitably to the children's sled, so this nineteenth-century sled developed into the modern Flexible Flyer. To the thin, flexible metal runners of the old timer, the modern sled adds a steering lever for better control while racing down snowy hills.

Little Red Sled

The graceful lines of an old sled have been carefully scaled down to produce this miniature, 5½″ × 6″ × 18″ model. Use it as the starting point of a table centerpiece or mantel decoration, filling it with fruit, nuts, cones, greens, or cookies. It would even make a planter if you line it with aluminum foil. The problems of assembly have also been scaled down to practically nothing. In fact, it's so simple that you might invite a child to join the project.

Materials and tools

¼″ plywood or pine.
¾″ brads.
Wood glue.
Non-toxic, red paint.
Sabre saw.
Sandpaper.
Hammer.

Directions

1. Enlarge the pattern pieces from the grid (see Skills Pages for instructions), and cut pieces out.
2. Remove any rough edges with sandpaper.
3. Temporarily assemble pieces in positions indicated at bottom of grid by nailing only enough to hold in place. When satisfied that everything fits, glue and nail pieces together. Countersink brads if desired.
4. Give the sled two coats of bright red paint. Be sure it is non-toxic if it will be given to a small child.

About "milk" paint

In the old days dried milk was used as a base thickener for paint. That gives old pieces their dusty color. Some colonial restoration areas such as Sturbridge Village or Colonial Williamsburg sell this paint in their gift shops. One manufacturer is The Old-Fashioned Milk Paint Co. Box 222, Groton, Mass. 01450.

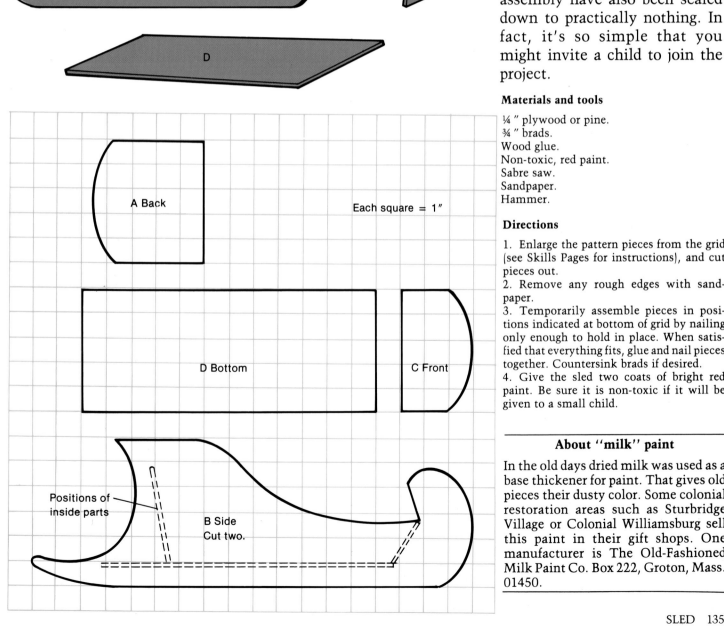

Marble Roller

Old-fashioned toys may not plug in and light up, but they *do* move. This marble roller, for example, uses gravity power to generate endless fascination. The marbles hurtle and rumble down an inclined pathway. Warning: once you start a handful of marbles rolling, you may not be able to tear yourself away.

Old-time clay marbles were smaller than modern glass ones and made a different sound.

Materials

1 x 1 lumber with groove routed for marble: 14 pieces 31¼" long; 1 piece 12" long (cut from five 8' lengths). (Ripping your own 1 x 1's from common lumber will save you money.)

1 x 4 lumber: 1 piece 31¼" long.

1 x 12 lumber: 1 piece 4' long.

2 or 3 large white plastic bleach bottles.

1¼" brads (for attaching 1 x 1's to the side pieces).

¼" tacks (for attaching deflectors to ends of the 1 x 1's).

1½" wood screws (for fastening back brace to sides).

Tack hammer and countersink punch.

Sabre saw.

Small quantity of wood stain.

Small paintbrush.

Sandpaper.

Instructions

1. Rout a groove on one side of each 8-ft. length of 1 x 1. Be sure to rout the groove wide enough so that the marble will touch the sides, but will not roll on the bottom of the groove. Next, cut 14 pieces that are 31¼ inches long and one piece that's 12 inches long. Gently smooth all of the pieces with sandpaper.   (1)

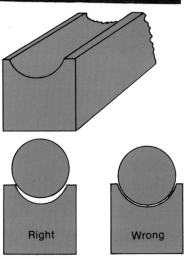

Right   Wrong

Groove in marble track

This marble roller is a replica of the original, which was designed and built in 1869 as a Christmas present for Annie P. Roundy, aged 3, by her uncle in Salem, Massachusetts. It has been passed down through four generations of children, fascinating those New England youngsters and whoever came to visit their families' homes. Old-fashioned detachable, stiff shirt collars (now tattered and turning brown) were tacked around the corners to keep the marbles rolling in the groove.

2. Refer to figure to see how to cut both sides of the marble roller from one 4-ft. length of 1 x 2. Draw the right and left side patterns onto the wood with a pencil. The sides can be laid out with a ruler and a carpenter's square from the dimensions given in figure. Cut out both sides very carefully with a sabre saw.

3. Cut a 31¼-in. back brace from 1 x 4 and attach it to each notched side with two 1½-in. wood screws.

4. Cut the back brace notch into the back edge of each side as shown in figure.

5. Using glue and 1¼-in. brads, attach a grooved track from the top of the left side to the top of the right side. Attach the next track from right to left, and so on.

6. Where tracks meet, trim the upper track edge with a sharp penknife so a marble will roll easily from the upper to the lower track.

7. After attaching the bottom (fourteenth) grooved track between the lowest right step and the lowest left step, nail and glue the 12-in. track so it slants downward toward the back of the left side. Trim the edge of the side track where it meets the bottom track so that a marble will roll easily from one to the other.

8. Apply wood stain to all of the wood surfaces with a small paintbrush and allow to dry thoroughly.

9. Cut 15 2″ × 4″ rectangles from white plastic bleach bottles and round two corners on one of the long sides as shown in figure.

10. Tack a deflector around the end of the top track and at each corner where the other track pieces meet (see photograph).

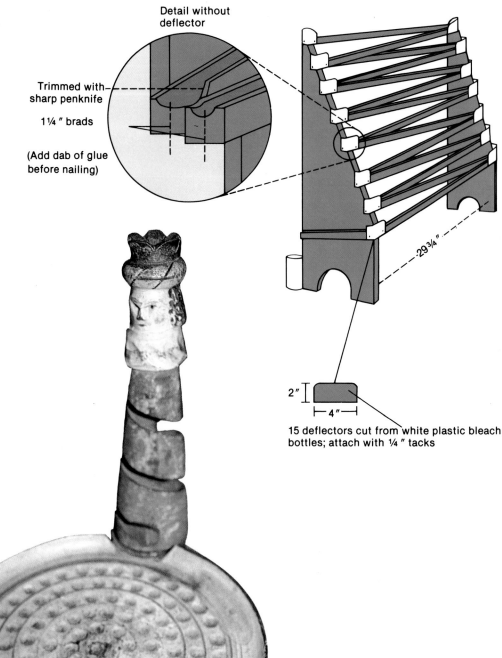

Detail without deflector

Trimmed with sharp penknife

1¼″ brads

(Add dab of glue before nailing)

29¾″

2″

4″

15 deflectors cut from white plastic bleach bottles; attach with ¼″ tacks

Toys that use marbles have always fascinated children if only for the movement and noise that they make. There seems to be something endlessly fascinating about feeding marbles in at the top and watching them shoot out at the bottom, as they do in this old, ceramic tower game.

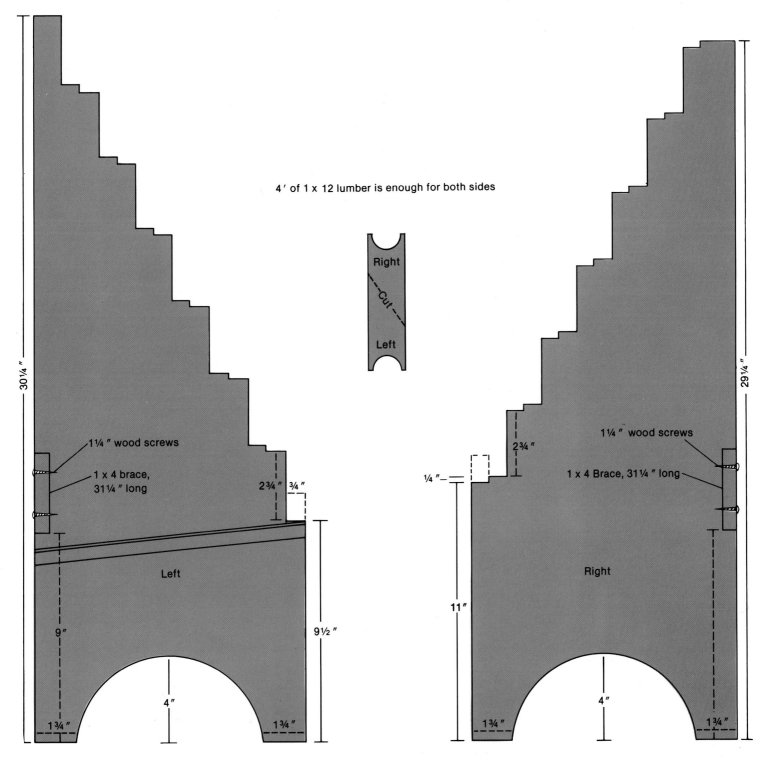

4′ of 1 x 12 lumber is enough for both sides

Right

Cut

Left

30¼″

1¼″ wood screws

1 x 4 brace, 31¼″ long

2¾″ ¾″

Left

9″

9½″

4″

1¾″ 1¾″

29¼″

1¼″ wood screws

2¾″

¼″

1 x 4 Brace, 31¼″ long

Right

11″

4″

1¾″ 1¾″

Christmas morning means toys under the tree, and that demands a place to put them when playtime is over. The toy train, rabbit pull toy, and the little wheel barrow, as well as the teddy bear and the doll (all made according to instructions included in this volume) will travel comfortably in the rolling toy chest shown on the opposite page.

Toy Chest

The toy chest is a rolling box that fits into a larger box. The larger "garage" is open at the bottom and one end. The chest is open at the top. It backs inside the garage, closing off the open end, to keep its cargo of toys out of sight. And it's sturdy enough for a four-year-old to ride in.

Materials

Plywood—¾" thick, 4' × 8'. This is a standard size sheet. Ask for ash or birch veneer core if you plan to stain it or use a natural finish. Veneer core is less expensive than solid wood core. Ash or birch on the outside show attractive grains that take stain evenly.

Lumber—approximately 6' of 1 × 8 board, which actually measures ¾" × 7¼", for the ladders, wheels, and finishing strips on the garage box.

Dowel—two 17½" lengths of ¾" (diameter) for the axles.

Rope—½" thick and 7' long.

Nails—about 6 doz. ½" finishing nails.

Two washers with holes at least ⅞" in diameter.

Acrylic enamel paint. The chest shown required a pint of red (two coats) for basic color and yellow, green, white, and blue for accents. If you want a natural wood finish, you'll also need stain and/or varnish for the outer garage.

Tools

Carpenter's square (an L-shaped steel ruler).

Electric sabre and circular saws OR hand rip and crosscut saws.

Electric or hand drill with ⅞", ½", and ¼" bits.

Hammer and a nail set (or a large 16d nail).

Sandpaper to erase marks and to round splintered or sharp edges before painting.

Here's a solution for the problem of what to do about all the scattered toys: the children will probably fight among themselves over whose turn it is to pull this boxy fire engine around the house and gather them in its capacious cargo hold. Then they can park the engine neatly out of the way in its own garage.

Cutting the pieces

When you build boxes, the measurements must be accurate and the corners square. Place a carpenter's square on the corners before you measure or cut. If the corners are not perfect right angles, trim the end to square them.

Mark the measurements of the cuts as you go. The easiest way to cut narrow strips is to start from the bottom and cut each strip in sequence to its full length. Then cut the strips across to make the component pieces.

1. Cut the pieces out of the 4' × 8' sheet of ¾-in. plywood. Use a power circular saw. Keep in mind that the actual dimensions of the pieces will be slightly less than shown because of the width of the saw cuts.

2. Cut the ¾-in. strips and 4½-in. wheels out of a 1 × 8 board, at least 6 feet long. Re-measure the big plywood panels after you have cut them and adjust the actual length of the strips, if necessary.

TIP: Add the thickness of the saw blade's cut each time you mark off a series of cuts and saw along the same side of the line each time.

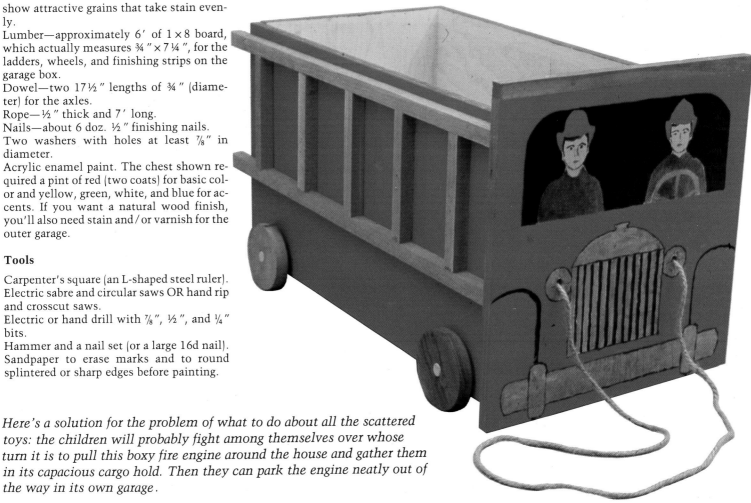

Assembling the truck

1. Drill ⅞-in. axle holes through the bottom corners of both of the side pieces, 2 inches from the bottom and 4 inches in from the ends.

2. Glue and nail the truck pieces together as shown. Be sure to set the floor piece at least 3½ inches up from the bottom so it will clear the axles.

3. Cut and insert the two 17½-in. axle dowels through the holes, slip on the washers and hammer the wheels on flush.

4. Paint the truck red. Paint the front panel with firemen, then nail it carefully on one end of the truck so that it will fit exactly into the open end of the garage when the truck is backed all the way in.

5. Round off the sharp rear corners of the ¾-in. strips for the 31-in. sides of the two ladders. Glue and nail them to the rungs. Nail them to the sides of the truck with the rounded ends sticking out in back.

6. Drill ½-in. or ⅝-in. holes through the painted headlights, all the way through both thicknesses so you can run the ends of the tow-rope through the holes and knot them inside.

7. Be sure the glue and paint have all dried overnight before you let your children get at it.

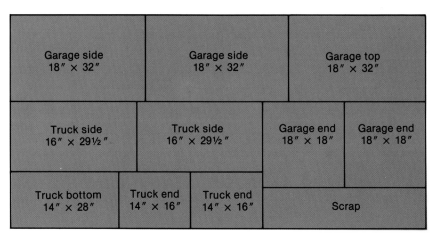

Cut these pieces for the garage-table and the fire truck toy box out of a standard 4′ × 8′ sheet of ¾-in. plywood. Actual dimensions may vary due to width of saw cuts.

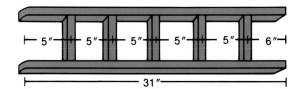

Assemble the two ladders made from ¾-in. strips and nail them to the sides of the truck.

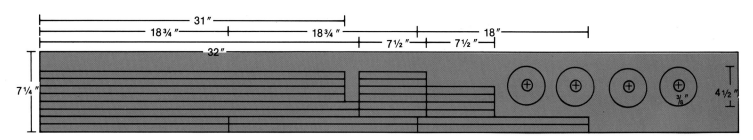

Cut these ¾-in. finishing strips, ladder pieces, and 4½-in. wheels out of a 1 × 8 solid board at least 6 feet long. (2)

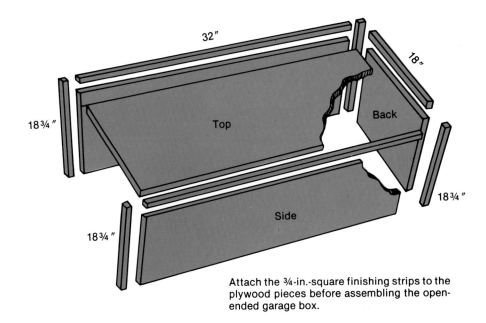

Attach the ¾-in.-square finishing strips to the plywood pieces before assembling the open-ended garage box.

Assembling the garage

1. Glue and then nail the 32-in. strips to the top edge of each of the two side pieces. Then glue and nail through the strips into the exposed ¾-in. edge of the top piece.

TIP: If you prefer the look of wood pegs covering the nail heads, see Figure 4.

2. To make the back of the garage, glue and nail an 18¾-in. strip on each exposed side edge of the 18″ × 18″ plywood back end. They will stick up ¾ in. above the top. Fit and fasten one 18-in. strip along the top edge of the back. Then glue and nail through the strips into the exposed ends of the top and sides of the garage.

3. Attach the remaining two 18¾-in. strips to the top of the front 18 in. × 18 in. plywood end piece. Lay it aside. It will be nailed to the front of the fire truck later.

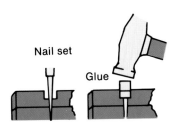

Drill ¼-in. holes about ¼ inch deep into the strips where the nails will go. Drive the nail in with a nail set, glue pieces of ¼-inch dowel into the holes, and sand the tops flush.

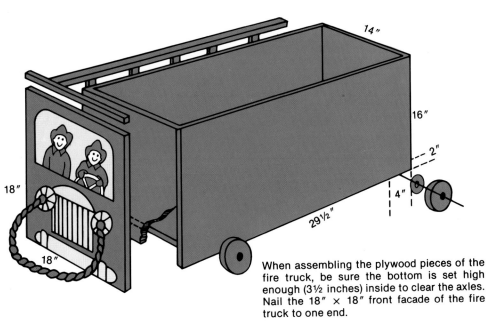

When assembling the plywood pieces of the fire truck, be sure the bottom is set high enough (3½ inches) inside to clear the axles. Nail the 18″ × 18″ front facade of the fire truck to one end.

TOY CHEST   143

HOLIDAY RECIPES

One of the greatest joys of the Christmas season is bringing together family and friends to share good times that will become traditions to remember and repeat. With good food to eat, songs to sing, and tales to tell, you can fill your gatherings with the warmth and cheer of a traditional country Christmas. Have a party for carolers, with nogs and grogs and other Christmas desserts, and sing carols in the moonlight with your home-made lantern to guide you on your way. The recipes and projects in this section will provide you with good fun, even before the season begins.

Decorative "show" towels were used by early Americans to cover up ordinary hand towels in the kitchen and bathroom. These are showing off Martha Washington's Great Cake. Martha may have kept her cake in a colorful tin box, served it on a carved wooden tray, or sliced it with an ivory-handled knife like the ones in this photograph. Husband George is depicted in the turn-of-the-century postcards in the foreground.

Chapter 5: Gifts from a Country Kitchen

To Make A Great Cake

Take 40 eggs & divide the whites from the yolks & beat them to a froth then work a pound of butter to a cream & put the whites of eggs to it a spoon full at a time till it is well work'd then put 4 pounds of sugar finely powdered to it in the same manner then put in the youlks [sic] of eggs & 5 pounds of fruit. 2 hours will bake it add to it half an ounce of mace & nutmeg half a pint of wine & some fresh brandy.

This was wrote by Martha Custis for her Grandmama.

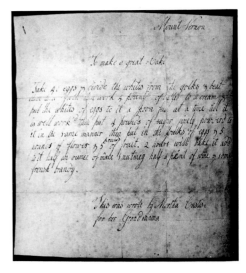

Martha Washington's and Other Great Fruitcakes

The kitchen wing of George and Martha Washington's mansion at Mount Vernon, Virginia, was built approximately fifteen years after they married in 1759. Most of the artifacts in this photograph date back to the period when the kitchen was used to prepare the family's meals. Some were actually used by the Washingtons' servants, such as the large marble mortar on the stool at right, and the pewter hot-water plates on the mantel, which kept the food warm while carrying it over to the main house. A "smoke jack" hangs from the mantel to the right of the fireplace. After being wound up as if it were a clock, it would—by the use of weights—release a fan from inside the chimney to clear out smoke. In addition, it could be rigged up to turn the spit over the fire at the same time. By performing the two jobs at one time, the cook could attend to other things, such as the time-consuming Great Cake (pictured on the previous pages). This was a cake that was served at Mount Vernon for Twelfth Night, Christmas, and many other "great" days of the year. Perhaps it was a recipe that Martha in-

vented as a young girl, since the hand-written copy shown is signed with her maiden name, Custis.

It isn't likely that cooks today will want to duplicate this particular recipe, which requires beating no less than forty eggs, so here's an adaptation that'll make you feel as though you've made the original cake. It calls for only those ingredients which would have been available in Martha Washington's day.

For optimum flavor, prepare to make the Great Cake *at least* one month in advance; the longer it has to mellow, the better it'll taste.

1 lb. golden raisins
1 11-oz. box currants
1 cup candied orange peel
¾ cup candied lemon peel
1 cup citron
⅓ cup candied angelica
⅓ cup each candied red and green cherries
½ cup brandy
4½ cups sifted all-purpose flour
1 teaspoon mace
½ teaspoon nutmeg
1 lb. (4 sticks) softened butter
2 cups sugar
10 (not 40!) eggs, separated
2 teaspoons fresh lemon juice
⅓ cup sherry

The night before baking

1. Pick over the raisins and currants and soak in water.
2. Chop orange and lemon peel quite fine. Do the same with the citron, angelica, and both kinds of cherries. Pour brandy over the fruit.
3. Allow all the above to stand overnight.

The day of baking

1. Preheat oven to 350°F. Grease and flour a 10-in. tube pan, a 10-in. Turk's-head mold, or 2 large loaf pans.
2. Sift together flour, mace, and nutmeg, then set aside.
3. Work butter until creamy, then add 1 cup of the sugar a little at a time. Beat until smooth.
4. Beat egg yolks until thick and light; beat in remaining cup of sugar a little at a time. Add lemon juice. Combine with the butter-sugar mixture.
5. Add flour mixture and sherry alternately. Stir in all of the fruit.
6. Fold in stiffly beaten egg whites. Pour batter into prepared pans.
7. Put a pan of hot water in the bottom of preheated oven; then, place the cake pans in and bake for 20 minutes. Reduce heat to 325°F and continue baking 1 hour and 40 minutes if it's a large cake, or 40 minutes for loaf cakes. Cakes are done when a toothpick, inserted at the center, comes out dry.
8. Turn baked cake out on a rack to cool; wrap in cheesecloth that's been soaked in sherry or brandy. Store in an airtight crock or tin for at least one month. If the cheesecloth dries out during this mellowing period, soak it again with the same spirits and rewrap the cake.

Fruitcakes ❄

Hints on Fruitcakes

Dried and candied fruits which characterize fruitcakes are a little difficult to cut up. For easier handling, dip your knife or scissors into water.

If baking at a high altitude, be sure to omit any leavening called for in the recipe.

Prepare cake pans (either loaf or tube) by lining them with greased wax paper.

After the cake has baked, let it cool in the pan for 20 to 30 minutes. Next, remove the waxed-paper lining and let the cake continue to cool on a wire rack.

Leftover fruits or nuts (or both) can be used to decorate the finished cake. Use thin sugar syrup to "glue" them to the cake or apply a thin icing layer to the entire cake and then stick the fruits and nuts to the surface.

For long-term storage (some say 25 years), be sure the cake is soaked in alcohol, then dredged in powdered sugar. Wrap in brandy- or wine-soaked linen towels, then aluminum foil. Place the cake in a tin with a tightly-fitted lid and store in a cool place. Seal the lid airtight with tape.

Dark Fruitcake

Rich and mellow with bourbon and wine, this recipe yields 12 pounds of fruitcake, enough to fill two loaf pans and two tube pans.

 4 cups all-purpose flour
 1 tablespoon cinnamon
 1 tablespoon cloves
 1 tablespoon allspice
 1 tablespoon nutmeg
 ½ tablespoon mace
 1½ teaspoons salt
 2½ lbs. currants
 2½ lbs. raisins
 1 lb. citron
 1 lb. pecan meats

 1 lb. + 2⅔ cups brown sugar
 1 lb. butter
 15 eggs, separated
 ¼ cup bourbon whiskey and ¼ cup wine (or ½ cup thick fruit juice, such as prune, apricot or grape)

1. Preheat oven to 275°F. Have all ingredients at room temperature before baking cake. Prepare pans by first greasing them, then flouring or lining with waxed paper.
2. Sift 3 cups of the flour with the spices. Set aside.
3. Wash the currants; cut up the raisins and citron; coarsely break the pecan meats. Stir all into the remaining 1 cup of flour.
4. Gradually add sugar to the butter, and cream the two until very light in color. Beat in the 15 egg yolks.
5. Add the flour to the butter mixture gradually, alternating with the bourbon and wine. Fold in the floured fruits and nuts.
6. Beat the 15 egg whites until stiff but not dry. Fold them into mixture.
7. Place a shallow pan filled with water into the oven and leave it until the last hour of baking. Pour batter into prepared pans and bake 3 to 4 hours for a 2½-pound cake, or 5 hours for a cake that's over 5 pounds.

Fruitcake Mocha

Just a hint of chocolate makes this fruitcake delectably different; as a final touch, glaze it with melted apple jelly.

 3 cups dark, seedless raisins
 1½ cups diced, candied citron
 1 cup candied cherries, halved
 1 cup diced, candied pineapple
 1 cup pecan halves
 1 cup slivered, blanched almonds
 1 cup dried currants
 ½ cup diced, candied orange peel
 ½ cup diced, candied lemon peel
 2 cups flour
 6 eggs, separated
 1 cup sugar
 1½ teaspoons ground cinnamon

 1½ teaspoons ground cloves
 1 teaspoon ground nutmeg
 ½ teaspoon baking soda
 1 cup shortening
 ½ square unsweetened chocolate, melted
 ¼ cup lemon juice
 ¼ cup orange juice
 ¼ cup apple jelly

1. Preheat oven to 300°F. Line a 10-inch tube pan with aluminum foil. Combine the fruit and nuts with a cup of the flour and coat them well. Set aside.
2. Beat egg whites until soft peaks form; add ½ cup of the sugar, 1 tablespoon at a time, and beat at high speed of mixer until whites stand up in stiff peaks.
3. In another bowl, mix 1 cup of the flour with ½ cup of the sugar, egg yolks, spices, shortening, chocolate, and juices; beat at high speed of mixer for 5 minutes.
4. Stir batter into fruit mixture; fold in egg whites. Pour into prepared pan. Bake 2 hours and 10 minutes or until done. On a wire rack, cool cake completely while in the pan. Remove from pan and peel off aluminum foil. Wrap cake and store until ready to serve.
5. Before serving, melt the apple jelly over low heat in saucepan. Brush on cake and let it set.

Fruitcake Tropicana

The kumquats and coconut add a distinctive, tropical taste to the classic, white fruitcake recipe.

 4 cups flour
 1⅓ cups pecans or hickory nuts
 1 cup blanched, slivered almonds
 2⅓ cups white raisins
 1⅓ cups seeded, chopped preserved kumquats
 1 teaspoon double-acting baking powder

½ teaspoon salt
2¾ cups butter
2 cups sugar
5 eggs
1 teaspoon vanilla
½ cup finely-sliced citron, candied orange peel or lemon peel
¼ cup chopped, candied pineapple
¼ cup chopped, candied cherries
½ cup finely-shredded coconut

1. Preheat oven to 350°F. Have all ingredients at room temperature before making cake.
2. Sift the flour. Extract ½ cup and mix it with 4 cups of the nuts and fruits. Set aside.
3. Resift remaining flour, the baking powder, and salt. Set aside.
4. Cream butter and sugar until light and fluffy; add the 5 eggs, one at a time, then the vanilla.
5. Stir the flour mixture into the butter/sugar/egg mixture until thoroughly blended. Fold in the remaining flour/nuts/fruit mixture.
6. Pour into two prepared 4 × 8½-in. loaf pans. Bake one hour.

"Canned" Fruitcake

Here's a recipe suitable for making small individual cakes for gifts. Simply use 10½-ounce soup cans as baking molds. Wash and dry the cans thoroughly; then grease and flour them just as you would prepare any other type of cake pan. The recipe makes 12 cans of golden fruitcakes.

4 cups sifted flour
2 teaspoons baking powder
2 teaspoons ground cinnamon
½ teaspoon ground nutmeg
½ teaspoon salt
2 cups butter or margarine
2 cups brown sugar
12 eggs
4 cups candied pineapple (cut up)
3 cups chopped pecans
1½ cups red, candied cherries (halves)
1 tablespoon grated lemon rind
Buttercream frosting (see recipe below)

1. Preheat oven to 275°F. Stir together the dry ingredients and set aside, reserving ⅓ cup.
2. Cream butter and sugar together. Add each egg individually and beat well after each addition. Gradually add the flour mixture, *except* for the reserved ⅓ cup. Mix thoroughly.
3. Combine the reserved ⅓-cup flour with the pineapple, pecans, cherries and lemon rind. Stir into the batter.
4. Spoon the batter into the prepared soup cans and fill to one inch from the top. Bake for 1 hour and 15 minutes, or until cake is done. Remove from the cans and let cool on racks.
5. Laying the cakes on their sides, ice with buttercream frosting. Cut candied fruits into flower shapes and use to decorate the cake.

Buttercream Icing

2 cups sifted, powdered sugar
1 tablespoon soft butter
1 tablespoon milk
½ teaspoon vanilla

Cream butter. Gradually add the powdered sugar. Add milk and vanilla and beat until smooth.

Fruitcake Cookies

Homemade Christmas cookies are always a welcome gift to receive. Here's a recipe that makes plenty. A variation of traditional fruitcake, these cookies can be stored in air-tight containers a month in advance.

4 cups dark molasses
1 cup brown sugar
1 cup margarine
2 eggs
½ lb. dark raisins
12 oz. mixed glazed fruit
4 oz. cooked pitted prunes
1 cup black walnuts
1 cup pecans
½ tablespoon lemon extract
1 teaspoon cinnamon
½ teaspoon nutmeg
½ teaspoon vanilla extract
1 cup apple butter
¼ cup baking soda
2 tablespoons evaporated milk
4 to 5 lbs. flour
Powdered confectioner's sugar or buttercream frosting (optional)

1. Preheat oven to 350°F. Choose a very large container for mixing the ingredients.
2. Blend together the molasses and brown sugar; beat in the margarine. Add the eggs, lemon and vanilla extracts, and mix until well blended.
3. Add the raisins, glazed fruit, prunes, and nuts, stirring well to moisten all of the ingredients.
4. In a small bowl, combine the cinnamon, nutmeg, and baking soda, making sure to press out any lumps. Add to the former mixture and stir well.
5. Add the apple butter and evaporated milk and blend well.
6. Add the flour, one cup at a time; until the dough is of a drop-cookie type of consistency. Drop by spoonfuls onto a *lightly* greased cookie sheet and bake for 12 minutes.
7. If desired, roll the baked cookies while they are warm in powdered sugar or glaze with a buttercream frosting. Makes approximately 200 cookies.

Cookies ❄

"Cookie," an American word, comes from the Dutch *"Koekje,"* which means "small cake." You will find that these small cakes are particularly appropriate to make for Christmas holidays. Here's why: they are quick and easy to make, especially fun for children to help with, lend themselves to a variety of holiday decorations, can be prepared well ahead of time and frozen 'til needed, are welcomed as gifts by many people (from doorman and newsboy to school teacher or tennis partner), and even hold up well (compared to a cake, for example) in the mail, if properly packed. The cookies in this section can become your basic, holiday assortment or can supplement your own favorites.

Enormous "lap" napkins once covered the expansive laps created by ladies' crinoline underskirts. Now that laps aren't so large, we use these beautiful old fabrics as small tablecloths. Artfully arranged on this one is a selection of classic cookies. They are, clockwise, starting in the left-hand corner: "Pennsylvania Slipware Cookies," served on a piece of authentic slipware pottery; "German Christmas Fruit Cookies," in an old, copper sieve; "Ginger Snaps" and "Heavenly Tarts," stacked on a carved, wooden-leaf tray; and "Oatmeal–Raisin Squares" and "Scotch Shortbread," sharing space in a rare, black-iron, wire tray. Served with coffee from the antique pewter pot in the background, these would please anyone.

Oatmeal–Raisin Squares

½ cup butter
1 cup (scant) brown sugar
½ teaspoon salt
1¼ cups flour
1¼ cups rolled oats
¾ teaspoon baking soda
¾ lb. raisins
1 cup water

1. Boil raisins and water for a few minutes. Let cool.
2. Cream together butter and sugar, using electric mixer on medium speed. Add salt, flour, oats, and baking soda.
3. Pat two-thirds of the oat mixture into an 8½ × 8½-in.-square pan. Spread raisin filling on top and remaining oat mixture on top of that. Press flat.
4. Bake at 400° for 20 minutes.

Scotch Shortbread

½ lb. butter (1 cup)
½ cup sugar
2½ cups sifted flour
¼ teaspoon salt
1 teaspoon vanilla extract

1. Combine all ingredients in a large mixing bowl. Knead with both hands into a large lump. Continue kneading about 5 minutes.
2. Flatten to ¼-in. thickness in a lightly-greased, 15¼ × 11-in. aluminum pan.
3. With a fork, press all around the edge and prick the entire surface of the shortbread.
4. Bake at 315° for approximately 18 minutes (to a light biscuit color). Cut into squares while still warm.

Oatmeal Lace Cookies

2 eggs
1 cup sugar
1 teaspoon salt
1 teaspoon vanilla extract
2 cups uncooked quick-cooking oats
2 teaspoons baking powder

1. Using electric mixer on medium speed, combine eggs, sugar, salt, and vanilla. Beat very well.
2. Add oats and baking powder, blending thoroughly.
3. Drop by *half* teaspoonfuls onto well-greased cookie sheet about 2 in. apart. Bake at 400° for 6 to 7 minutes. Cool cookies a magic few seconds before lifting from pan.
Makes 50 to 60 cookies.

Ginger Snaps

1 cup sugar
1 cup (scant) shortening
1 egg
4 tablespoons molasses
2 cups flour
2 teaspoons baking soda
1 teaspoon ginger
1 teaspoon cinnamon

1. Cream together sugar and shortening, using electric mixer on medium speed. Add egg and molasses and mix well.
2. Combine dry ingredients and blend into sugar mixture.
3. Set the dough aside to "rest" for an hour or two. Then roll into balls the size of large marbles.
4. Place on greased cookie sheet and bake at 325° for 10 to 12 minutes. Makes a jillion.

Christmas Sugar Cookies

3 cups sugar
¾ lb. (1½ cups) butter
3 eggs
4 cups flour

1. Cream together sugar and butter until smooth, using electric mixer at medium speed.
2. Add eggs, mixing after each.
3. Fold in flour until blended. Dough should be firm but of a manageable consistency.
4. On lightly floured surface, roll the dough out to ¼-in. thickness.
5. Cut the dough with floured cookie cutters into various shapes. You can, of course, create shapes of your own with a sharp knife.
6. Bake at 375° for 5 to 8 minutes, until a light golden brown. Be careful, because they burn easily.

Pennsylvania Slipware Cookies

1½ cups butter
1 cup sugar
2 eggs
1 teaspoon grated lemon rind
4½ cups sifted flour
¼ teaspoon salt
food colors

1. Cream together butter and sugar in bowl until light and fluffy, using electric mixer at medium speed. Add eggs and lemon rind; beat well.
2. Sift together flour and salt; add gradually to the creamed mixture.
3. Starting with ½ teaspoon each, add red and green food colors to make a rich, brown batter.
4. Cover and refrigerate dough 3 to 4 hours.
5. Roll out a portion of dough on lightly floured surface to ⅛-in thickness. Using a small saucer as a guide, cut in circles. Place on greased baking sheet.
6. Bake in 400° oven 6 to 8 minutes or until golden brown.
7. To decorate cookies: Make one recipe of "Decorator Frosting" (see "Gingerbread Farm" project). Add small amount of water, if necessary, to make it the consistency of chocolate syrup. Add red and yellow food colors to make frosting a warm yellow (should roughly match the authentic slipware plate pictured here). With a small brush, free-hand paint any design you like on the cookies: names, flowers, starts, curlicues, etc.

Heavenly Tarts

1 cup butter
4 tablespoons sifted confectioners' sugar
1 teaspoon vanilla extract
3 teaspoons water
2 cups flour
1 cup chopped pecans and/or almonds
confectioners' sugar

This piece of Pennsylvania Slipware pottery will serve as a guide for decorating slipware cookies. The cutters on the shelf above would be perfect for "Christmas Sugar Cookies."

1. Cream butter, confectioners' sugar, vanilla, and water, using electric mixer on medium speed.
2. Slowly add flour and nuts.
3. Shape small finger-length cookies and place them on ungreased baking sheet.
4. Bake at 300° for 35 to 40 minutes.
5. Roll in confectioners' sugar, cool, and roll again.

German Christmas Fruit Cookies

2 cups honey or light corn syrup
⅔ cup (scant) brown sugar
½ cup margarine or butter
1 egg
¼ lb. dark raisins
6 ozs. mixed, glazed fruit
2 ozs. cooked, pitted prunes
½ cup black walnuts
½ cup pecans
¾ teaspoon lemon extract
½ teaspoon cinnamon
¼ teaspoon nutmeg
¼ teaspoon vanilla
½ cup apple butter
1½ teaspoons baking soda
1 tablespoon evaporated milk
2–2½ lbs. flour

1. Mix all ingredients, except flour, in a large container. Add flour until dough is the consistency of drop cookies (about 2¼ cups flour).

2. Drop by teaspoonsful onto baking sheet and bake at 350° for about 12 minutes.

3. Roll in confectioners' sugar while warm or glaze with a thin mixture of confectioners' sugar and water. These cookies may be prepared a month ahead of time and stored in airtight containers. Include apple slices to retain moisture. Makes 100 cookies

Candies ❄

The history of candy is the history of sugar, first refined by the Arabs, later brought to the New World by none other than Christopher Columbus. Here, as elsewhere in the world, candy-making was at first the province of druggists because it was thought that certain ingredients (peppermint, hoarhound, wintergreen) had healing properties. Now we know that candy has no medicinal—in fact, no nutritional—value, except as a source of quick energy. It is eaten for pure pleasure. Appropriately, it has taken a place among traditional holiday pleasures.

When making the candies in this section, allow plenty of time for cooking and cooling, both of which may take longer than you imagine. Use: large, heavy pots; long-handled, wooden spoons for stirring; and a candy thermometer (if you don't have one, use the cold-water testing method described in the recipes). Follow directions exactly: Don't take shortcuts. Don't double recipes or make substitutions. Pay particularly close attention to the last few minutes of cooking when temperatures rise quickly. Most candies do not freeze well. Store different types separately in airtight containers.

The little bird in the background, a charming piece of early-American folk art, seems to be about to sample the ''Poppycock'' in this photograph. Clockwise, the other sweets, delectably displayed on an old pine table (note the wooden pegs), are: ''Spiced Pecans,'' ''Holiday Rum Balls,'' and ''Chocolate–Nut Squares.''

Poppycock

1½ cups sugar
½ cup light corn syrup
½ cup water
½ teaspoon salt
8 cups popped popcorn
1 cup toasted almonds, pecans, or peanuts
2 tablespoons butter
1 teaspoon vanilla extract

1. Combine sugar, corn syrup, water, and salt. Cook over low heat, stirring constantly, until sugar dissolves.
2. Cook over medium heat to hard-crack stage (300°), or until small amount dropped into cold water forms hard threads.
3. Meanwhile, spread popcorn and nuts into a buttered jelly-roll pan and heat in oven at 350° for 10 minutes.
4. Remove syrup from heat and quickly stir in butter and vanilla extract until butter melts. Pour over popcorn mixture. Stir to coat well.
5. Spread in thin layer on a flat surface. Cool and separate into clusters. Makes 2 quarts

Date Loaf-Candy

2 cups sugar
1 cup milk
1 tablespoon butter
1 teaspoon vanilla extract
½ lb chopped dates
2 cups chopped pecans

1. Boil sugar, milk, and butter until syrup forms a soft ball when dropped into cold water.
2. Add dates and cook until tender (5 to 10 minutes).
3. Remove from heat; add vanilla extract and pecans. Beat until stiff.
4. Pour onto a damp cloth and shape into a roll.
5. Chill. Wrap in foil and refrigerate until ready to slice. You can refrigerate this for months, but do not freeze.

Spiced Pecans

1 cup sugar
½ cup water
¼ teaspoon cream of tartar
¼ teaspoon cloves
½ teaspoon cinnamon
½ teaspoon nutmeg
½ teaspoon salt
2 cups pecans

1. Boil sugar, water and spices to the soft-ball stage, that is, until the syrup forms a soft ball when dropped into cold water. Add pecans.
2. Turn out on buttered, waxed paper and separate nuts so they don't remain in clusters. Let cool.

Old-English Nut Toffee

1 lb. (2 cups) butter
4 cups sifted sugar
2 cups finely chopped nuts
1 lb. milk chocolate
    butter

1. In a heavy, 3-qt. saucepan, melt butter; add sugar and 1 cup nuts.
2. Place over medium heat and bring to a boil, stirring constantly, until mixture reaches 212° on a candy thermometer. Then, without stirring, continue to cook over low heat until thermometer reads 300°. If butter separates or candy browns too rapidly on the sides, *do* stir briefly.
3. When mixture reaches 300°, stir gently for a few seconds, then pour at once onto a cool, buttered marble slab or on several buttered cookie sheets. Spread out until candy is ⅛ to ¼ in. thick.
4. Allow to stand a few minutes, then loosen bottom.
5. Melt milk chocolate in top half of a double boiler.
6. When toffee is cold, break up. Cover with melted milk chocolate and remaining nuts. Be sure chocolate has hardened before storing. Toffee will keep several weeks in an airtight tin.

Holiday Rum Balls

3 cups crushed vanilla wafers
1 cup confectioners' sugar
2 tablespoons cocoa
3 tablespoons corn syrup
6 tablespoons rum
1 cup finely chopped nuts
    confectioners' sugar

1. In a bowl, mix vanilla wafers, 1 cup confectioners' sugar, and cocoa.
2. Add corn syrup, rum, and nuts. Mix together. If necessary add a few drops of water so mixture holds together.
3. Pinch off small amounts of mixture and roll into balls. Roll in confectioners' sugar.
4. Let stand 60 minutes, and roll in sugar a second time. Store in covered container for 2 or 3 days before serving. Makes 3- to 4-dozen rum balls

Chocolate–Nut Squares

2 squares unsweetened chocolate
½ cup (¼ lb.) butter
1 cup sugar
½ teaspoon salt
1 teaspon vanilla extract
2 eggs
½ cup sifted flour
½ cup chopped nuts

1. In top half of a double boiler, melt chocolate and butter together.
2. Add successively: sugar, salt, vanilla, eggs (one at a time), and flour. Mix well.
3. Pour batter into greased shallow baking pan (approximately 15 × 10 in.) Pat nuts firmly on top.
4. Bake at 425° for 15 minutes; cut while still warm.

Chocolate–Mint Sticks

1 batch "Chocolate–Nut Squares"
batter.
½ teaspoon peppermint flavoring
½ cup chopped almonds or walnuts
2 tablespoons butter or margarine
1 tablespoon heavy cream
1 cup sifted confectioners' sugar
1 tablespoon peppermint flavoring

1 square unsweetened chocolate
1 tablespoon butter

1. To the batter for "Chocolate-Nut Squares," add ½ teaspoon peppermint flavoring and chopped nuts.
2. Bake at 350° for 25 minutes in a 9 × 9-in. baking pan. Let cool on rack.

3. Cream together 2 tablespoons butter or margarine, cream, confectioners' sugar, and 1 tablespoon peppermint flavoring for frosting. Spread on cake.
4. Let the frosting harden. Melt together chocolate and 1 tablespoon butter. Spread on top of peppermint frosting. Chill and cut into oblongs.

Candlelight and candies lend warmth and richness to any holiday coffee-and-dessert get-together.

Napkin Shapes

Napkins can be used to add a decorative, even elegant, touch to the dinner table, as well as hold small gifts or favors on Christmas or other special occasions. Here are three distinctive ways of folding them.

The Candle

The Candle is a simple shape that looks appropriate with modern as well as traditional china and glasswear. This versatile fold can be placed in the center of or above the plate. For a buffet, a group of napkins folded into candles makes a nice sculptured addition to the table.

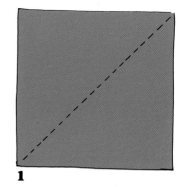

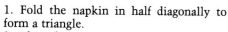

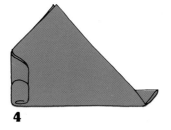

1. Fold the napkin in half diagonally to form a triangle.
2. Place the napkin so the fold is along the bottom edge.
3. Fold up the bottom edge about one and one-half inches.
4. Turn the napkin over and roll it up fairly tightly.
5. Stand the candle up and tuck the corner into the cuff to hold the rolled shape in place. If you like, fold down one layer at the tip of the candle to resemble a flickering flame.

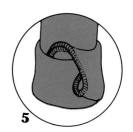

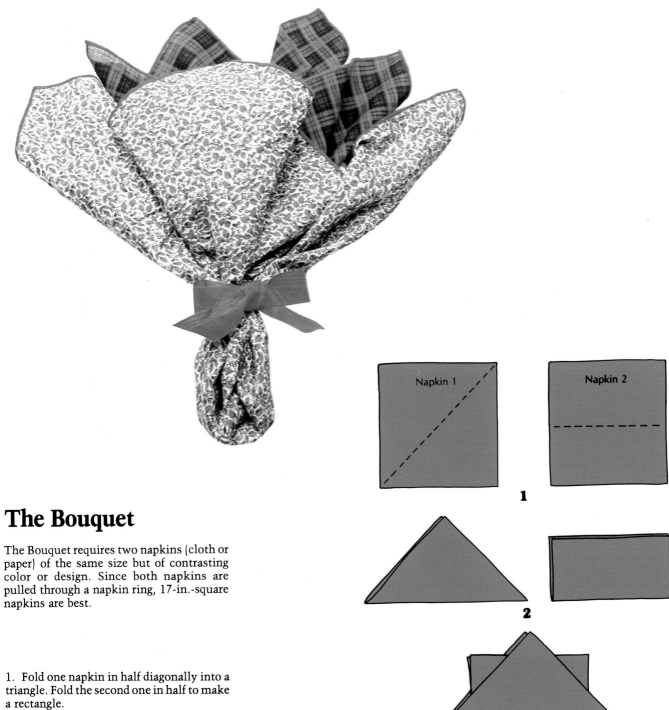

The Bouquet

The Bouquet requires two napkins (cloth or paper) of the same size but of contrasting color or design. Since both napkins are pulled through a napkin ring, 17-in.-square napkins are best.

1. Fold one napkin in half diagonally into a triangle. Fold the second one in half to make a rectangle.
2. Place the napkins so the folds are along the bottom edges.
3. Open the triangle and place the rectangle inside it. Hold the napkins together at the center of the bottom edge as you pull the bottom three inches through a napkin ring.

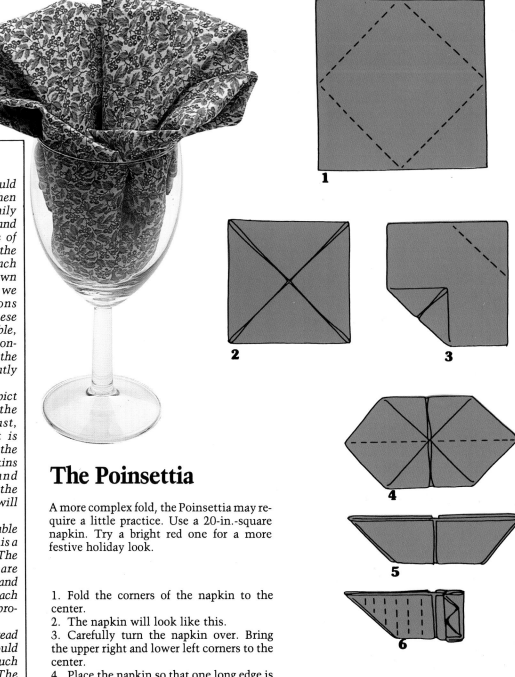

Serviettes

The Poinsettia

A more complex fold, the Poinsettia may require a little practice. Use a 20-in.-square napkin. Try a bright red one for a more festive holiday look.

1. Fold the corners of the napkin to the center.
2. The napkin will look like this.
3. Carefully turn the napkin over. Bring the upper right and lower left corners to the center.
4. Place the napkin so that one long edge is at the bottom.
5. Fold the napkin in half by bringing the top edge down to the bottom edge.
6. Accordion-pleat this shape into 1-in. pleats.
7. Place the bottom edge of the napkin in a glass. To curve the top, pull out and down on the left and right sides. To form the front petals, pull down on the free corners of the napkin at the center.

Skills Pages ❊

In this section you'll find explanations of some of the basic skills needed to complete crafts projects in this book. The subjects covered include:

How to Enlarge Designs and Patterns

Sewing Techniques: Hemming
                       Mitering
                       Clipping seams
                       Blind appliqué

Needlework Techniques: Needlepoint stitches
                           Needlepoint alphabet
                           Crewel stitches

Blocking and Framing Embroidery

Braiding for Mats and Rugs

Basic Woodworking

How to Enlarge Designs and Patterns

When the pattern or design for the parts of a project is larger than can be accommodated on the book's page, a scaled-down version is printed with a superimposed grid that looks like graph paper.

The instructional text and the legend on the grid will say, for example, "Each square = 1". This means, simply, that no matter what the size of the grid squares, each one represents one inch of actual size in the project. If the grid squares are ⅛" and the legend reads, "Each square = 1", then the actual parts will be eight times larger than they appear in the patterns. If the legend reads, "Each square = ½", then the parts will be four times larger than the patterns.

To make an enlargement of a gridded design or pattern with a specified enlargement scale, follow these steps:
1. Lay out your own graph paper or purchase some with the correct size larger grid squares.
2. Count the number of squares the smaller design covers from side to side and top to bottom, and mark off the same number of squares on the larger grid. Put dots at the corners of the rectangular area on the larger grid.
3. To enlarge the design, copy the pattern lines from the smaller grid to the larger grid, one square at a time. Use a ruler to transfer the straight lines and a French curve or a compass to reproduce curved lines. When all the lines are transferred, the enlarged pattern is ready to use.

If a design you wish to enlarge has no grid, you can apply your own over a tracing of the shape, set your enlarging scale, and then proceed to enlarge the design proportionally as described above. When choosing what grid size to place over the smaller design, use a larger grid (½- or 1-inch) for simpler shapes and a finer grid (⅛- or ¼-inch) for more complex designs.

Sewing Techniques

Hemming

1. Pin and baste the hem at the desired length. If you wish to miter the corners, see the instructions which follow.
2. Thread a needle with thread that matches your fabric.
3. With the piece wrong side up and the hem edge toward you, fasten the thread inside the hem crease.
4. Working from right to left, take a small stitch (through just one or two threads of fabric) in the piece itself, then slide the needle along ⅛ in. to ¼ in. inside the fold of the hem.
5. Continue around the piece, making sure you keep the stitches even.
6. Fasten the last stitch by sewing several stitches on top of each other, then run the thread through the hem and clip it off.

Mitering

Mitering the hem of a needlework piece gives a finished, neat look to a tablecloth, runner, or wall hanging.
1. Press creases of the desired width along the inside and outside hem lines A and B. (1)
2. Unfold the hem and clip off the corners on the diagonal (dotted line).
3. Turn down the corners. Refold the hem along lines A and B. (2)
4. Pin, baste and sew the hem, working a slipstitch along each miter at the corner. (3)

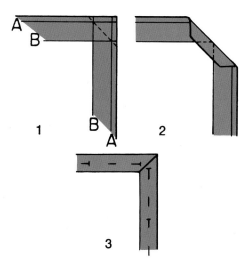

Clipping seams

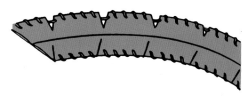

Curved seams must be clipped so that they will lie flat. After sewing, clip to about ⅛" from the seam in both pieces of fabric every inch or so, depending on the tightness of the curve. Outer curves should be "notched," as in the diagram. The seams may then be pressed open, as shown here, or pressed to one side and the edges overcast.

Blind appliqué

With sewing thread and needle, stitch the applique pieces in place using the blind hem stitch or slip stitch. The choice of stitches is not as important as the neatness and even length of the stitches. The edges of the applique pieces may then be decorated with embroidery stitches, such as chain stitch or feather stitch, but they are usually left plain.

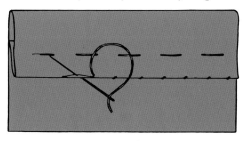

blind hem stitch

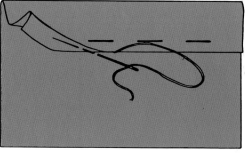

slip stitch

Needlework Techniques

Needlepoint stitches

General Instructions: Use yarn no longer than 18″. Repeatedly pulling a longer length through the canvas will fray and break it. The design areas may be worked first and the background filled in later. If you are working from a chart, it will be easier to work the needlepoint row by row, however.

Begin a new yarn by making a knot. Leaving knot on right side, run yarn down through canvas about 1″ from where you want to begin. Bring needle up at starting point. After the stitches worked later cover the loose end of yarn, clip off the knot. When ending a length of yarn, run it back under a few stitches on wrong side of work.

Half Cross-Stitch: The simplest of all needlepoint stitches is the half cross-stitch which is always worked from left to right. Start at the bottom of a stitch. Cross over 1 mesh of the canvas (diagonally) and insert needle down and through for next stitch. The needle is always inserted vertically. When the row of stitches is completed, turn work upside down so that next row can be worked from left to right.

Cross-Stitch: When a slightly more textured effect is desired, cross-stitch is often used for needlepoint. In working designs each cross-stitch is completed individually. On backgrounds, however, a row of half cross-stitch is completed, then the second half of the stitch is completed on the return. In either case the stitches must all cross in the same direction.

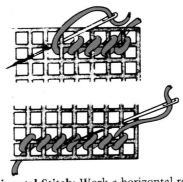

Continental Stitch: Work a horizontal row completely across from right to left; then turn the canvas upside-down, and work back across.

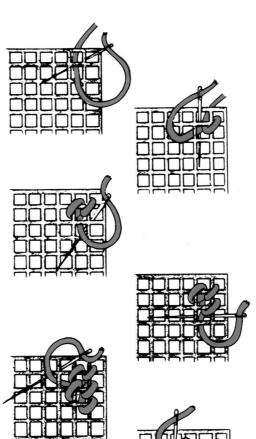

Basketweave Stitch: Work diagonally up and down; the stitches on the back of the canvas form a woven pattern.

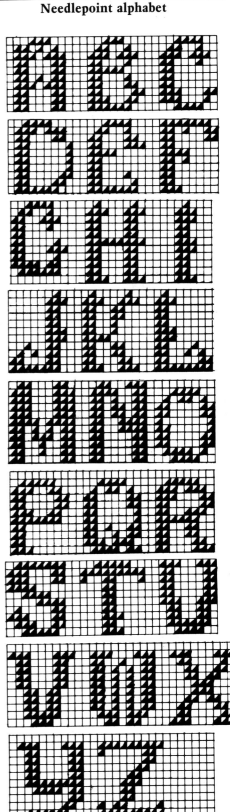

Crewel stitches

A piece of crewel work may be embroidered in only one basic stitch or in dozens of different stitches. Practice a few simple stitches to get the feeling of the work; later on you can enlarge your repertoire. First, on scrap fabric of an appropriate weight, draw some dots and straight lines; then, using your thimble as a guide, draw some curved lines and circles. Put the fabric in a hoop and, with whatever fine yarn or embroidery thread you have handy, practice some of the stitches shown here. For professional looking embroidery it is important to keep the stitches all the same length when working any given stitch.

Coral Stitch: This stitch is used for lines, for outlines and sometimes as filling. Work from right to left. Bring needle up at end of line to be embroidered. Hold down thread with left thumb, then make a tiny slanting stitch across line. Draw needle under and over thread as shown.

Cross-Stitch: This stitch is usually worked on crosses drawn on the fabric or on fabric which has threads that can be counted easily. Starting at lower left corner of a stitch and working from left to right, make a diagonal stitch (half cross-stitch) to upper right corner. Continue across, making a row of slanting stitches each going over an equal number of threads or over transferred pattern. Work back over these stitches as shown. You can work each cross-stitch individually and in any direction but they must all cross in the same direction.

Holbein Stitch: This stitch is used for lines and outlines. It is often used to outline solid areas of cross-stitch. Work running stitch along line to be covered, making sure that each stitch and space between stitches are all of equal size. Then work running stitch back over this line, filling in the empty spaces.

Laid Stitch: This stitch is a thread-saving way to fill in larger areas of a design. Make a long, straight stitch across the area. Instead of bringing thread under fabric and back to starting edge (as far "satin" stitch) make next stitch as shown, leaving size of a stitch between the two. Work all across the area, then fill open spaces with another series of stitches.

Star Filling Stitch: This stitch is used for rather open filling of an area or combined with other stitches. Work a cross-stitch on the straight rather than the diagonal. Then work another cross-stitch of equal size right over the first one, this time placing it on the diagonal. Finally, work a tiny cross-stitch in the center over the intersection of the first two.

Straight Stitch: This stitch is used as an occasional single stitch scattered in a design or grouped in a ring to form a flower. Each stitch is always separated from the·next one.

Blocking and Framing Embroidery

Laundering

If the finished piece needs cleaning, wash it in cold water with mild soap. Handle it gently; rinse thoroughly. Roll it in a towel to remove excess moisture. Then iron it dry, covering the front of the work with a handkerchief. Iron mostly on the back.

Blocking

Blocking your needlework will give it a fresh, finished look and prepare it for framing. With the piece still in the embroidery frame, wet a clean cloth and lay it on the right side of the needlework. Remove the cloth when dry.

To block after washing embroidery

1. Mount a piece of heavy paper on a large board and draw the exact outside size of your work on the paper.
2. While the embroidered piece is still wet but not dripping, fasten it to the board at each corner and then at the center of each side with rust-proof push pins or thumb tacks.
3. Continue adding pins halfway between those already in place until you have placed pins no more than ½-in. apart all around the piece.
4. Allow the piece to dry completely.

Mounting and framing

Whether you made your embroidery to fit a frame you already had or you purchased a new frame, it should be large enough to allow some plain background fabric to extend beyond the embroidered area. Traditionally, the fabric border is of equal width on the top and the sides but slightly wider at the bottom of the piece. But you can use your own judgment.
1. Remove any hardware on the back of the frame. Refinish the frame if you so desire.
2. Cut a piece of mat board to fit the desired frame size; center the embroidery on the white side of the board and draw the excess fabric over it. If there is more than 1½ to 2 inches of extra fabric, trim it off. (1)

3. Fasten the fabric to the edges of the board with straight pins; make sure the threads of the background fabric line up squarely with the edges of the board. (2)

4. Fold the corners under and stitch the edges together with strong thread. (3)(4)

5. Lace the edges of the fabric together with long strands of strong thread. Remove the pins. (5)

6. Clean the glass and insert it in the frame. Put the picture in the frame face-down and anchor it by carefully hammering a fine wire nail into the center of each side of the rabbet.

Note: For a large frame, you will need two or three nails on each side.

7. If you wish to protect the back of the needlework piece, cut a sheet of brown paper to cover the entire back, glue it to the frame and trim it flush with the frame.

8. Replace any hardware on the back of the frame.

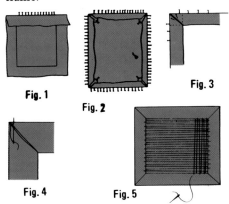

Fig. 1   Fig. 2   Fig. 3
Fig. 4   Fig. 5

Braiding for Mats and Rugs

1. To prepare fabric for braiding, cut or tear strips 1″ to 1½″ wide; cut on the crosswise grain so that the strips will have more give and lie flat. Trim the ends of the strips on the diagonal and sew them together. When estimating the amount of fabric needed, remember that strips will lose one-third to one-half their length when braided.

2. Turn the cut edges of each strip to the center on one side and fold the strip in half to enclose them. Each strip is now four layers thick and will make an even braid. To make a finished end for starting a three-strand braid, sew the ends of two braiding strips together on a diagonal, and fold the strip as just described. Insert the end of a third folded strip at the point of the seam

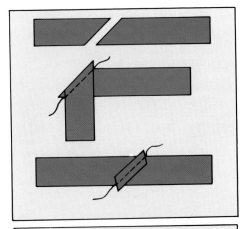

and pin it in place to form a T. Then begin braiding by folding the top right strand down over the center strand.

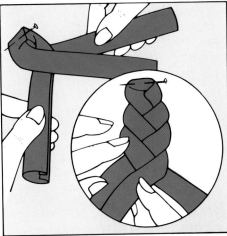

3. Continue braiding by folding the left strand over the center strand. Make sure that the open side of each strip faces the right at all times. Do not fold the strips over when working them from one side of the braid to the other. This will produce a firm, uniform braid and a reversible rug.

Hints: If the seams on all three strands fall at the same place in the braid, repiece at least one strand to avoid a bulge. When adding strips or putting the work down, hold the braid tight with a safety pin or a large paper clip.

Basic Woodworking

Here's some straightforward advice for beginners on the basics—woods, tools and fasteners. You can cut it, hit the nail on the head, and get it all together once you understand the characteristics of wood, how to select and use the proper tools, and how to choose the right fasteners and adhesives.

Wood

Types

Wood can be broadly classified into hardwoods and softwoods. Oak is a hardwood, and so are pecan and dogwood. Common softwoods are pine, fir, western cedar and redwood. Softwoods have varying degrees of strength and hardness. White pine and fir are easy and inexpensive softwoods to work with. Yellow pine is a stronger softwood, but has a greater tendency to split and crack than other softwoods such as western cedar or redwood.

Plywood is made with thin sheets of wood (called veneer) glued together under pressure. The grain runs in alternate directions on each of these sheets. This makes plywood stronger than a solid wood board, hence better for most furniture and large construction projects.

Chipboard (or particle board) is made from wood chips glued together. It is less expensive but breaks more readily than solid wood or plywood. Use it only for projects that will not be subjected to stress.

Grades

The terms No. 1 and No. 2 "common" refer to the clearness of solid wood boards. No. 1 is virtually knotfree, while No. 2 has some knots. If you select No. 2 carefully, you get good wood for significantly less money than No. 1.

Plywood panels are stamped with code letters A, B, C, or D to indicate grades of beauty and amount of faults. A-D grade means it is good on one side and not so good on the other.

Sizes

Wood is sold either by the board foot or linear length. A board foot consists of the physical dimensions of 12 by 12 by 1-inch thick. A board 12 by 12 by 2-inches thick would contain two board feet. Wood trim pieces are sold by the linear foot.

Lumber, when originally sawn at the mill, is rough cut to the specified dimensions you pay for. But then it is planed on all four sides to smooth the surface and eliminate saw marks, thus reducing its size before it is marketed. For example, when you ask for a solid board 1-inch thick by 1-foot wide, you actually get a board that is ¾-inch thick by 11¼ inches to 11½ inches wide. A 2 x 4 board is actually 1½ by 3½ inches. Plywood and particle boards, however, are cut and sold to the same exact dimensions.

Grain

The direction in which the grain (darker stripes) runs in a board determines its strong and weak points.

If you place a board so the support is with the grain, the weak spot is the center of the board, and it's likely to break easily. Support it against the grain for strong construction.

Sanding

Garnet sandpaper is the best for wood projects. Aluminum oxide is better for metal, and silicon carbide will sand glass and metal.

Sandpaper is graded extra fine, fine, medium, coarse, and extra coarse. Medium and fine are most useful; coarse, only for very rough surfaces, or to remove finishes.

The best way to hand-sand a flat surface smooth is to wrap the sandpaper around a wood block which you can hold in your hand. Hold fast with thumbtacks and sand the wood surface back and forth with the grain. Sanding against the grain will leave scratches which will show when you finish the wood.

Tools

Most beginning projects can be made with small, hand power tools. In general, you will be better off spending more money to get the top of the line. The right tool, well made, will help you do a neater job faster.

You will be less likely to waste materials and you'll be more pleased with your finished projects.

Hammers

They may not look different, but they are. A curved claw hammer that weighs about 13 oz. and has a solid wood or fiberglass handle is the best size for both men and women in light woodworking. Use a 16 oz. hammer for large construction projects requiring thick lumber and large nails. The face of the hammerhead should have a slight outward curvature for consistently straight driving action. Don't use heavy blows when striking a nail. Position the hammer squarely over the nail and hit it with a short, sharp swing, mostly with your wrist—so that the handle of the hammer ends up at right angles to the nail.

Saws

A good saw is worth the investment because it will hold its edge and cut faster and truer under a wider variety of conditions. A good hand saw will do most jobs. Two of the most useful types are a coping saw and a crosscut saw—ask for a "fine-cut" blade.

Don't force a saw. Let a good, sharp blade do the work for you.
TIP: If the wood is green or sticky, apply mineral spirits to the blade to lubricate the cutting action.

A power sabre saw is probably the most useful, versatile tool for a beginner. Most home craftspeople will also eventually want a circular saw with a carbide-tipped blade, for larger projects. A sabre saw with a variable speed control in the trigger will give you better control and accuracy for cutting both straight lines and curves. A "skip-tooth" or, "plywood," blade gives the smoothest cut under most conditions. If your sabre saw tends to jump up and down, make sure that the saw's cutting platform is flat on the wood. Apply medium downward and forward pressure on the handle and hold your work piece firmly.
TIP: The trick to cutting a straight line with a power saw is simple: make a guide by tacking a narrow, straight-edged strip of wood on the waste side of the cut, parallel to your cutting line. Keep the saw's cutting platform pressed against it as you cut.

Drills

In selecting an electric drill, look for one with a ¼-in. chuck (one that will hold a drill bit with up to a ¼-in. diameter shank). A ¼-in. drill that has a variable speed feature and a reverse switch is a good investment. It

spins at a speed of 2000 to 2500 rpm, and there are some optional attachments that only work effectively at those speeds (circle-cutting and sanding attachments, for example). The variable speed and reverse action are ideal for setting and removing screws. The slower speeds allow you to drill into hard materials.

"Spade" bits are better for fine cabinet making than the more common "twist metal" drill bits, which tend to mar the edges of the hole somewhat more. Other useful but inexpensive attachments that save time are a circle cutter, screwdriver bits, and a buffer/sander.

Routers

They carve all kinds of grooves in wood with different blades to make decorative moldings, fancy edges around decoupage plaques, and fancy joints for furniture.

Electric hand-held routers are expensive ($30 to over $100), but are fast and surprisingly easy to operate (as with all power tools, wear safety glasses and don't wear loose-fitting clothing).

The higher the speed (revolutions per minute), the easier it is to make a smooth cut with one pass. A good combination for the money is ½ horsepower with 28,000 rpm. Look for these features:

☐ Easily located and activated on-off switch.

☐ Convenient installation and removal of interchangeable bits.

☐ Accurate, firmly clamped depth adjustment.

☐ A ball-bearing motor that can take the high speeds.

☐ Optional attachments including an edge-guide and a circle cutter.

Such a wide variety of bits and knives are available to cut different shapes that, even though kits are generally cheaper than buying the elements separately, you may be better off building a collection of the shapes you like. Ogee or cove mold bits are frequently used for the edges of decoupage plaques.

Screwdrivers

Woodworking with only one screwdriver available is as frustrating as driving a car on one cylinder. A short stubby screwdriver can go where your fist fits. Long shanks provide greater twisting power. Fat handles take better advantage of your gripping strength. Some screwdrivers are made with a flat section in the shank that you can grip with pliers or a wrench to increase gripping power.

Always pre-drill screw holes slightly smaller than the screw's threads in hardwood, and in softwoods only half as deep as the threaded portion of the screw.

Match the width of the screwdriver blade to the slot in the screw. It should not be wider than the slot because it will mar the surface of the wood when you twist the screw down flush. If the blade is narrower, it may bend or jump out of the slot, because the sides of the blade take the twisting pressure. A screwdriver with a ¼-inch blade will probably be the handiest size.

Phillips head screws (with a deep cross in the head instead of one slot) require a matching screwdriver. They are easier to drive with a power screwdriver.

Planes, rasps, and files

A plane is a hand tool that shaves wood to reduce its thickness or to even a rough surface. A "jack" plane that is 2 to 2¼ inches wide and 7 to 8 inches long is the most useful for general light woodworking. Keep the blade sharp and practice with it on the surface of scrap wood before you dig into something that counts.

Rasps and files are used mostly for rounding edges, shaping contours and removing waste stock. A rasp is bigger than a file and has rows of serrated cutting teeth where a file has fine grooves. The most useful rasp for home woodworking is a forming tool with handles over a flat replaceable cutting surface. It will do some of the wood shaving jobs a small plane will do, and is easier for a beginner to operate successfully. Files are used for finer finishing work.

Measures and squares

We are heading toward the metric system, so look for measures that show both inches and feet and metric centimeters and meters.

Tapes: A ¾-inch-wide steel tape will hold up longer than a ½-inch tape. The slight extra cost of a 16-foot versus a 12-foot length is worth it in convenience.

Rulers: Use a metal ruler for accuracy. A rubber, felt or cork backing will keep it from slipping and raise it up slightly so a cutting tool won't ride into it. Eighteen inches is a handy length.

TIP: Use a wooden yardstick, like the ones lumberyards sometimes give away, for drawing circles by drilling a small hole at each inch interval. To draw a 24-inch diameter circle, for example, tack a small nail through the 1-inch hole and into the board. Put a pencil point through the hole at 13 inches, and swing the yardstick around the nail.

Squares: An accurate square is essential for wood construction projects because the pieces will not fit properly when you assemble them if the angles at the corners are not exact.

The most useful squares are a small try square (inexpensive, used for squaring off the ends of boards); large steel carpenter's square (doubles as a measure, useful for measuring pieces to be cut from sheets of plywood).

Fasteners

Two keys to fastening wood firmly without splitting it are to choose the correct size nails or screws (the thinnest and shortest possible), and to pre-drill screw holes.

A rule of thumb for length is: the fastener should equal the thickness of the first board plus one half to three quarters of the thickness of the second board. Select the thinnest finishing nail or screw you can get in the proper length.

Nails

Most nails are measured and sold in "pennys," written "d," because "d" used to be the British monetary symbol for penny. For example a 10-penny nail, written "10d," is three inches long and could be used to nail two 2 in. by 4 in. boards together. Ask for rust-resistant aluminum or galvanized nails for outdoor work.

Finishing nails are headless and thin for their length. They are used for fine work where the pieces are apt to be thinner and the heads are normally recessed slightly below the surface.

Nail sets

Setting (recessing) finishing (small headed) nails just below the surface of the wood is an essential step in making a smooth finished product. Nail sets come with tips to fit different sized nails, so they will not mar the wood.

Screws

Use screws when there may be twisting or pulling stresses on the piece, when you may want to take it apart later, or for fine decorative work where you don't want hammer marks or the head to show. Ask for wood screws. The threads on "sheet-metal" screws are different. Flat heads are best for fine work because they fit flush with, or below, the surface (be sure your screwdriver blade is not wider than the slot). They come with a normal single-slotted head or an x-slotted Phillips head which is easier to fit a drill bit into.

The diameter of screws is measured in seemingly arbitrary gauge numbers, like wire. Use the chart to find the gauge number of the size you will need.

TIP: Because screws are thick, always pre-drill the hole. Use a bit slightly smaller than the diameter of the screw and slightly shallower than its length.

Countersinking

Recessing finishing nails and screws slightly below the surface of the wood is essential for fine work. Drive a finishing nail almost to the wood so the hammer doesn't mar the surface. Then drive it barely below the surface with a nail set. (The point of a 16d nail will do in a pinch.)

To countersink flat-headed, wood screws, enlarge the very top of the pre-drilled hole with a tapered countersink bit the same diameter as the screw head.

TIP: To give the work a wooden-peg look, sink the screw well below the surface (about ¼ in.), cut a slice of wood dowel of the same diameter but slightly longer than the depth of the hole. Fasten it in the hole with a drop of glue and sand the peg even with the surface.

Adhesives

To save time and provide a stronger finished product, always glue pieces together—even if you also fasten them with nails or screws. Most brands of glue fall into one of the following categories:

White glue (polyvinyl acetate)—good for most jobs. Clamp with medium pressure.

Aliphatic resin—excellent for woodworking, semi-waterproof, sets relatively fast.

Resorcinal—good, waterproof.

Epoxy—for non-porous materials.

Hide and casein glues—good.

Plastic resin—excellent, waterproof, expecially for outdoor work.

Contact cement—only for attaching sheet materials (veneers, plastics) to wood.

Stain Removal Chart

Stain	Washable fabrics	Dry-clean fabrics
Alcoholic beverages, soft drinks, wine	On a fresh stain, sponge with cold water. On a stain that has dried, soak in cold water. Then wash in warm water using soap or detergent.	On a fresh stain, sprinkle immediately with cornstarch until the liquid is absorbed. On a dry stain, sponge with cold water.
Ballpoint pen	Place paper towels under the napkin and sponge with denatured alcohol. Each time you apply more alcohol, move the stain to a clean part of the paper towels. Then launder using bleach if the napkin is white.	At the dry cleaner's specify that the stain was made by a ballpoint pen.
Berries and other fruits, fruit juices	Sprinkle immediately with salt to absorb the liquid. Apply white vinegar to the stain before laundering.	Follow the instructions for washable fabrics but after treating the stain, send the napkin to the dry cleaner's.
Candle wax	Rub wax with an ice cube until hard, then scrape off with a blunt knife. Or, place paper towels under and over the napkin and press with a warm iron. Change the paper towels frequently until all the wax has been absorbed by the towels.	Follow the instructions for washable fabrics. If after removing the wax, a stain remains rub with cleaning fluid.
Catsup, tomato sauce	Soak in warm water and liquid detergent, then launder using bleach if possible.	At the dry cleaner's, specify that the stain is tomato sauce.
Chewing gum	Rub with an ice cube, then scrape off with a blunt knife.	Follow instructions for washable fabrics.
Chocolate, coffee, tea	Sponge with cleaning fluid. Let the napkin dry, then launder using bleach if possible.	At the dry-cleaner's, specify the source of the stain.

Stain	Washable fabrics	Dryclean fabrics
Ink	Pour water through the napkin until the water runs clear. Then apply detergent and white vinegar. Rinse well.	Follow the instructions for washable fabrics.
Lipstick and other cosmetics	Rub the stain with detergent dissolved in lukewarm water, then launder.	Use a greasy stain solvent, then dry-clean.
Mildew	Launder, then dry in the sunlight.	Dry-clean, then air in the sunlight.
Milk, cream, ice cream, butter	Soak immediately in cold water, then rinse thoroughly. Launder.	Sprinkle immediately with cornstarch. Allow the napkin to dry thoroughly, then brush the powder away.
Mustard	Soak in cold water and detergent or a soaking product. Then launder.	At the dry-cleaner's, specify that the stain is mustard.
Pencil	Erase with a soft eraser. Work detergent into any remaining stain. Then launder.	Erase with a soft eraser, then dry-clean.
Protein such as egg, meat, meat juice, gravy, blood	Soak in cold water. If the stain is still visible, sponge with cleaning fluid. Allow to dry before laundering.	Sponge with cold water; use cleaning fluid if necessary. Dry-clean.
Scorch	Sponge with hydrogen peroxide or ammonia. Rinse well and launder.	Dampen with hydrogen peroxide until stain is removed.
Vomit	Soak in a salt-water solution (one-quarter cup salt to one quart water). Launder.	Follow the instructions for washable fabrics, then dry-clean.